THE BENEFIT OF DOUBT WORKBOOK

HOW CONFRONTING YOUR DEEPEST QUESTIONS CAN LEAD TO A RICHER FAITH

WORKBOOK | 10 LESSONS

CRAIG GROESCHEL WITH DUDLEY DELFFS

HarperChristian Resources

CONTENTS

Introduction: Permission to Doubt v

PART 1: DEALING WITH DOUBT

LESSON 1:   Is It Wrong to Have Doubts? 3

LESSON 2:   Is What I Believe Biblical? 17

PART 2: OUR DOUBTS

LESSON 3:   Why Should I Believe God Is Good? 31

LESSON 4:   Why Doesn't God Answer My Prayers? 43

LESSON 5:   Why Would God Only Provide One Way? 55

LESSON 6:   Why Believe in Jesus When His Followers Are Such Hypocrites? ... 67

LESSON 7:   Why Does God Feel So Far Away? 79

LESSON 8:   Why Would God Send People to Hell? 91

LESSON 9:   Why Believe the Bible If Science Contradicts It? ... 103

LESSON 10: Why Would God Love *Me*? 115

Conclusion: Giving God the Benefit of the Doubt 125

Leader's Guide 127

About the Author 131

PERMISSION TO DOUBT

T*he Benefit of Doubt*. Maybe you paused when you read that title and wondered if that's really a thing. Can doubt actually have a *benefit*? After all, doubt is typically viewed in a negative light. We're told it implies a lack of confidence on our part. An uncertainty in our convictions. A lack of strength in our resolve. And when it comes to doubts regarding our *faith*—well, the message we usually receive is that we shouldn't go there. *Don't question . . . just believe.*

The reality, however, is that doubt is not your enemy. Rather, when you take the appropriate steps to work through your spiritual doubts, you will develop a deeper understanding and a more authentic relationship with God. Your doubts can actually lead you to a richer faith and be a great benefit in your spiritual walk.

This idea of embracing your doubts might cause you to feel uneasy. Perhaps you're afraid that if you examine your doubts too closely, it will lead you down the slippery slope to skepticism (or even cynicism). Or maybe you worry that your doubts will poke holes in some of your long-held beliefs. Or perhaps you are concerned that if you have doubts—and express them openly—it might cause those who look up to you to also begin to doubt. You may fear that your doubts could become contagious and infect their thinking as well.

The truth is that closely examining your doubts will likely not lead you to cynicism but to the ability to better understand why you believe what you do. Your doubts may indeed poke holes in some of your long-held beliefs—but instead of patching the holes, you'll get to press in to discover what *you* believe about God, not what others have told you to believe. And those who look up to you will benefit by knowing you have doubts you're not afraid to confront. It will encourage them to wrestle with their own doubts.

Virtually everyone, from the committed Christian to the hardcore atheist, struggles with doubt at times. What is important is not that you *have* doubts but what you *do* with those doubts. If you choose to ignore them, what began as benign uncertainty can metastasize into a destructive mindset that resists believing in anything—that slippery slope we mentioned to cynicism. But if you are willing to honestly address your spiritual doubts, you will find a greater capacity for knowing and loving God.

As a companion to *The Benefit of Doubt*, this workbook is an invitation for you to reconsider doubt as an integral part of your spiritual journey. It is intended to help you wrestle with your doubts—whether individually or with others in a small group—toward the goal of pursuing a richer faith. While no one can promise that you will never doubt again, the hope is that your doubts don't become a destination but a doorway to a more intimate relationship with God.

God *welcomes* your doubts. So, no matter what questions you're asking or how loud your doubts shout, you can take them to Jesus—for the first time or the hundredth time. If you seek the truth with an open mind, a tender heart, and a willing spirit, God will meet you there.

So don't be afraid to doubt. Take a deep breath, and let's get started.

DEALING WITH DOUBT

Facing your doubts so that you can grow in your faith may sound counterintuitive. You might worry about doubting to the point of wandering too far from your touchstones of truth. But the Bible reveals that dealing with doubt is part of being human—and part of developing a genuine relationship with God that can endure life's twists and turns. God not only permits us to have doubts but also reveals himself when we seek him with open hearts. Rather than ignoring, compartmentalizing, or fearing your doubts, you can push through them to find a foundation of God's truth for assessing your beliefs. Here are the key principles you will explore in part 1:

- Your doubt doesn't disappoint God.
- Your doubt doesn't define God—or define you.
- Your doubt doesn't deny your faith or disqualify you from ministry.
- Your doubts may be driven by circumstances, intellect, emotion, or other people.
- Your doubts may be driven by misperceptions and false assumptions about God based on your relationship with your earthly parents.
- Your doubts may be driven by your personality as well as by the choices you make and habits you develop.
- You can't have a reconstruction of your faith without a deconstruction of your beliefs.

IS IT WRONG TO HAVE DOUBTS?

The strongest faith isn't a faith that never doubts.
Rather, the strongest faith is a faith that grows through doubts.

CRAIG GROESCHEL

Having doubts about your faith can be a lonely experience. Even when you know that other people doubt, you might still be reluctant to voice your doubts for fear of what others will think. You've probably witnessed those who've expressed their doubts being shut down, whether in a casual conversation, a small-group gathering, or a Bible study. This is unfortunate because these should be safe places to air your doubts without fear of judgment.

While it might be helpful to know that people beside you in church have doubts, it can be even more helpful to know that some of history's most renowned Christians had doubts. People like Martin Luther, the father of the Protestant Reformation, who not only questioned the theology and practices of the Roman

Catholic Church in the sixteenth century but who also continued to have doubts about his salvation throughout much of his lifetime.[1]

Or take C. S. Lewis, the great twentieth-century apologist and author of iconic classics like *Mere Christianity*, *The Screwtape Letters*, and The Chronicles of Narnia. As an academic professor, Lewis continued to wrestle with doubt intellectually. The problem of loss, suffering, and grief was not simply philosophical and theological but deeply personal for Lewis, who married late in life and then lost his wife to cancer. Even as he became known as one of the great apologists for the Christian faith, Lewis had to keep working through his own questions.[2]

Then there's Mother Teresa, who was known for her commitment to serving the impoverished and those with severe medical ailments. She mostly kept her doubts private during her lifetime, but after her death in 1997, her diaries and journals revealed a believer brokenhearted by her lack of intimacy with God. Many people found her candor relatable and her faith even more admirable. She clearly continued living out her commitment to love and serve God even in the midst of lonely bouts that left her questioning her relationship with him.[3]

Numerous other famous followers of Jesus experienced doubt even while serving, ministering, preaching, and teaching—including John Calvin, Charles Spurgeon, and Pope Francis. These believers exercised their faith by trusting God and living out his calling on their lives even in the midst of their unanswered questions. They learned to accept doubt as a necessary part of their spiritual growth.

In the same way, rather than allowing doubt to undermine our faith, we're called to trust that God will meet us in the midst of our struggles. Doubt only becomes a problem when we're unwilling to push through it. Having doubts about your faith doesn't mean you're a bad Christian. Having doubts about your faith means you're in good company!

◆ Who has influenced you when it comes to expressing your doubts? How would you summarize your general attitude toward doubt until now?

◆ How does your doubt contribute to feelings of loneliness or isolation? When have you remained silent rather than express a doubt about matters of faith?

◆ What difference does it make in knowing most believers experience doubt at times? What's your reaction to the doubts experienced by well-known Christians?

◆ Which well-known Christian's life has inspired you in your faith journey? What do you know about how he or she handled times of doubt?

EXPLORING THE TRUTH

We've established that it's not wrong to have doubts. But that doesn't mean you've immediately identified, clarified, rectified, and welcomed your doubts as a gateway to a richer walk with Jesus. You're probably still harboring nagging doubts about doubt, wondering if it's really okay to express your feelings, and asking how your doubts can grow your faith.

This sense of unease about leaning in to your doubts makes perfect sense. If "faith is confidence in what we hope for and assurance about what we do not see" (Hebrews 11:1), then it's natural to assume that *lacking confidence* in what you hope for and *wanting assurance* for what you do not see must mean that you're a bad Christian.

This is simply not true!

Consider the story of perhaps the best-known doubter in the Bible: Thomas. He was one of the twelve disciples who was handpicked by Jesus and is often remembered mostly for . . . well, doubting. But if we look at how he became known as the original "Doubting Thomas," we quickly realize that he got a bad rap.

After Jesus' resurrection, Thomas wanted to be certain that his Master had returned to life in a body that was not only flesh and blood but also bore the scars of the crucifixion. Basically, he wanted more than secondhand testimony from the other disciples. He wanted *firsthand* evidence in order to believe what was humanly impossible. As you read the passage below, imagine how you would have responded if you had missed out on witnessing the presence of Jesus after he rose from the grave—and then received a second chance.

> [19] *On the evening of that first day of the week, when the disciples were together, with the doors locked for fear of the Jewish leaders, Jesus came and stood among them and said, "Peace be with you!"* [20] *After he said this, he showed them his hands and side. The disciples were overjoyed when they saw the Lord.*
>
> [21] *Again Jesus said, "Peace be with you! As the Father has sent me, I am sending you."* [22] *And with that he breathed on them and said, "Receive the Holy Spirit.* [23] *If you forgive anyone's sins, their sins are forgiven; if you do not forgive them, they are not forgiven."*
>
> [24] *Now Thomas (also known as Didymus), one of the Twelve, was not with the disciples when Jesus came.* [25] *So the other disciples told him, "We have seen the Lord!"*
>
> *But he said to them, "Unless I see the nail marks in his hands and put my finger where the nails were, and put my hand into his side, I will not believe."*
>
> [26] *A week later his disciples were in the house again, and Thomas was with them. Though the doors were locked, Jesus came and stood among them and said, "Peace be with you!"* [27] *Then he said to Thomas, "Put your finger here; see my hands. Reach out your hand and put it into my side. Stop doubting and believe."*
>
> [28] *Thomas said to him, "My Lord and my God!"*
>
> [29] *Then Jesus told him, "Because you have seen me, you have believed; blessed are those who have not seen and yet have believed."*
>
> JOHN 20:19–29

◆ How does Thomas's response to the other disciples' statement, "We have seen the Lord" (verse 25), reflect the way that you might have responded if you had been in his place? Do you usually believe what others close to you tell you, or do you need to decide for yourself?

◆ How do you typically respond when others ask you to provide proof about something? How does that compare to the way Jesus responded to Thomas?

◆ What might Thomas have been thinking when Jesus offered to let him touch his wounds? How would you have responded in this situation?

◆ Notice that Jesus didn't tell Thomas simply to "stop doubting." What did Jesus say to him right before he said that phrase—and then right after? How does Jesus' response to Thomas color the way you view doubting?

QUESTIONING THE TRUTH

The interaction Thomas had with Jesus makes it clear that we never have to feel ashamed of having doubts. Thomas wasn't being difficult or seeking extra attention—he was merely being honest about wanting evidence before he bought in to the resurrection. Nor was the doubt Thomas expressed an indicator that his commitment to Jesus was weak, half-hearted, or fickle. If we back up before this post-resurrection scene, we find that Thomas displayed boldness, courage, and a fearless attitude in his dedication to Christ.

In fact, based on what we find in the Gospels, Thomas might have been one of the most faithful followers of Jesus. In one story, Mary and Martha, the sisters of Jesus' friend Lazarus, sent word that Lazarus was sick. When Jesus heard this news, he remained where he was for two days, and then said, "Let us go back to Judea" (John 11:7). Now, there was a good reason for Jesus and the disciples *not* to go back to Judea. The Jewish religious leaders there were looking for Jesus and intended to kill him. The disciples pointed out this fact to Jesus, but their concern didn't slow him down.

The disciples knew that to accompany their Master back to Judea meant that they might be killed as well. It was a sobering possibility that surely made them all think twice—well, all except for one. As we read, "Then Thomas (also known as Didymus) said to the rest of the disciples, 'Let us also go, that we may die with him'" (verse 16).

There is no doubt here about Thomas's courage, conviction, and commitment. He wasn't afraid to speak up and express his willingness to face whatever Jesus was about to face. Nothing is mentioned about the other disciples saying anything in solidarity. Thomas didn't waver or hide—he displayed a kind of "risk everything" faith without hesitation.

Let's also remember that Thomas kept hanging out with his fellow disciples even after he expressed his desire for tactile proof of the risen Savior. Even though Thomas needed more than the others' testimony of the risen Lord (see John 20:25), he didn't abandon hope. In fact, we are told, "A week later his disciples were in the house again, and Thomas was with them" (verse 26). Thomas didn't have the firsthand evidence he needed yet, *but he still showed up.*

And by showing up, Thomas received what he needed in order to believe! Jesus not only appeared again to the disciples but also offered Thomas the opportunity to place his finger in the nail scars and his hand in Jesus' side where the soldier's sword had been. Jesus stood close to Thomas and told him to touch his wounds. Jesus didn't rebuke Thomas, shame him for doubting, or denounce his faith because he wanted tangible evidence.

God is willing to meet *you* in the midst of your doubts as well. He does not distance himself or abandon you for doubting. While you might feel disconnected from God in the midst of your questions, uncertainties, and doubts, he is still right there with you. He is willing to be touched, provide the evidence you need, and offer you reassurance of his presence. So don't stop seeking God when you have doubts but dare to trust that he is willing to meet you right where you are. He can handle your questions, fears, and frustrations.

The story of Thomas shows us that Jesus invites us to be honest with him, because sincere faith gets strengthened by doubts.

◆ What evidence is found in the story told in John 11:1–16 that Thomas was a faithful follower of Jesus?

◆ What is significant about the fact that Thomas remained in close contact with the other disciples even after expressing his doubt? What does this say about the importance of continuing to show up even when you have doubts?

◆ What stands out to you in the way that Jesus responded to Thomas? How would you like Jesus to respond to your doubts and desire for reassurance?

◆ What specific questions continue to nag at you in the midst of your faith journey? Which one troubles you the most at a personal level? Why?

DIGGING DEEPER INTO DOUBT

Thomas wasn't the only follower of Jesus who had doubts. Even some who had encountered the risen Son of God after the resurrection still doubted. And those two times when Jesus crashed his disciples' gatherings in the upper room were not his only post-resurrection appearances—not by a long shot. The New Testament mentions more than a dozen times when Jesus appeared to his followers after the resurrection and before his ascension to heaven.

The women outside his empty tomb met him (see Matthew 28:8–10), as did two men walking to Emmaus (see Luke 24:13–35). Ten of the disciples (meeting without Thomas) saw Jesus as they were hiding from the Jewish leaders (see John 20:19–25). When some of them later went fishing, they encountered Jesus on the beach (see John 21:1–23). Christ even appeared before five hundred people at one time (see 1 Corinthians 15:6).

In Jesus' final appearance before the ascension, he instructed the disciples to meet him on a mountain so he could give them their assignment: to go into all the world and share the good news of the gospel (see Matthew 28:19). But this scene wasn't tied up with a bow. Even though the eleven remaining disciples met up with Jesus, right before he gave them the Great Commission, there is a detail that must not be overlooked: "When they saw him, they worshiped him; *but some doubted*" (verse 17, emphasis added).

Yep, these were the disciples who knew Jesus intimately and had been with him for the past three years of his ministry. They had not only witnessed his betrayal (by one of their own, no less) and his arrest and torturous death—but they had encountered him in the flesh when he rose from the grave. And yet . . . some *doubted*? It's easy to imagine they worshiped him—but some still doubted. Maybe even some who worshiped him had doubts.

The details included in the Bible are not just random, anything-goes, whatever-they-remembered-at-the-time details. So, if Matthew mentioned that some of the disciples doubted here in the final moments before Jesus ascended into heaven, its significance can't be ignored. Remember, the Bible offers us an accurate account of history, often written by eyewitnesses to the events. We're not told all the details and descriptions that we might like, but when one catches our attention like this one, we can safely assume it matters.

It matters in this case because if Jesus' early disciples had doubts while standing right in front of him, it's understandable if we doubt at times—we who can't phyiscally see and touch him. Notice in this story that Jesus didn't rebuke the doubters and thank the worshipers. Instead, he told them *all* to go and share the gospel—including those who still doubted. Jesus knew that some were doubting, but he didn't disqualify them from being his followers because of it. He understood that *doubt offers an invitation to a deeper faith*.

As you consider how your doubts can invite you to a richer relationship with God, it might be helpful to examine the basis for your doubts. With this goal in mind, use the following categories and questions to help you assess what's attached to the doubts you hold.

DOUBTS BASED ON CIRCUMSTANCES, PAST EXPERIENCES, AND EMOTIONS

◆ How have your most painful losses and disappointments contributed to the doubts you have? What questions do these experiences raise?

◆ What recent personal circumstances tilt you toward doubting? What feelings and assumptions emerge when these doubts arise?

DOUBTS BASED ON INTELLECT AND IDEAS YOU HOLD

◆ Generally, are you persuaded more by rational evidence or by your feelings and intuition? How does this tendency affect your spiritual doubts?

◆ What are some of the questions and concerns you have about the Bible? How do these influence your willingness to rely on it as your source of God's truth?

DOUBTS BASED ON (AND INHERITED FROM) OTHER PEOPLE

◆ Which family members have most influenced your views on God, faith, and Christianity? What role have your friends played in your beliefs or doubts?

◆ Which pastors, teachers, and leaders have had the greatest impact on your faith? What did you learn about the role of doubt from them?

DOUBTS BASED ON MISPERCEPTIONS AND FALSE ASSUMPTIONS ABOUT GOD AND THE BIBLE

◆ What image of God did you form while you were growing up? What was the basis for this image and perception of him?

◆ How has your relationship with your parents or early caregivers influenced the way you see God now? What false assumptions and biases might have arisen because of this?

DOUBTFUL AT BEST

Your doubts offer an opportunity to deepen your faith, which in turn grows stronger and helps you push through those doubts. It would be nice if the stronger your faith gets, the fewer doubts you have—and if that's your experience, count your blessings. But experiencing a closer relationship with God doesn't necessarily guarantee that you won't still have doubts from time to time. Like the first disciples, you can worship Jesus and still have doubts.

This tension results from the fact that no matter how strong your faith becomes, you still live in a broken world. You'll find a similar dynamic at work in many aspects of living out a commitment to Christ. Experiencing God's peace doesn't mean you will escape the chaos in the world. Receiving his love doesn't mean you won't have struggles in this world. Basking in his joy doesn't mean you will never have a bad day. However, what you *will* have is God's presence in the ups and downs of life. You can experience his peace, love, and joy despite your circumstances. Similarly, you can exercise faith despite the doubts you encounter.

Perhaps nowhere in Scripture is this tension expressed more poetically than in the Psalms. One of the best-known and most beloved of them, Psalm 23, describes how you can experience God's love, protection, rest, and provision even in the midst of unwanted challenges: "Even though I walk through the valley of the shadow of death, I will fear no evil, for you are with me" (verse 4 ESV). In the next verse, the psalmist addresses this awareness once again: "You prepare a table before me in the presence of my enemies" (verse 5).

Having doubts doesn't mean you don't also have faith. When you're walking through dark valleys, you keep walking and take comfort in knowing that God is with you. You don't have to be afraid, because God's presence is greater than any evil the enemy throws in your path. Similarly, you can experience the kind of divine intimacy that comes from being a beloved guest at God's table—even while your enemies are still present.

Learning to recognize this tension allows you to reconsider your doubts, and as you reframe them within a more accurate context, you can see their benefits. So, based on what you read in chapter 1 of *The Benefit of Doubt*, as well as the doubts you identified from the end of that chapter and the exercise in this lesson, it's now time to dig deeper into what these doubts can reveal to you about your beliefs, their basis, and potential benefits.

While it might be tempting to list every doubt you've ever had in your life, consider sticking with the ones that presently trouble you or continue to linger—perhaps the "top ten" on your list. Be completely honest in your response even if these doubts seem irrational, subjective, inherited from others, or trivial. Try not to judge yourself for having doubts but instead let yourself be curious about them. Be a doubt detective as you explore each one.

DOUBTS YOU HAVE	BASIS OF THIS DOUBT	BENEFIT OF THIS DOUBT
1.		
2.		
3.		
4.		
5.		
6.		
7.		
8.		
9.		
10.		

NOTES
1. Jesse Carey, "Seven Prominent Christian Thinkers Who Wrestled with Doubt," Relevant, June 9, 2021, https://relevantmagazine.com/faith/seven-prominent-christian-thinkers-who-wrestled-doubt/.
2. Carey, "Seven Prominent Christian Thinkers Who Wrestled with Doubt."
3. Carey, "Seven Prominent Christian Thinkers Who Wrestled with Doubt."

IS WHAT I BELIEVE BIBLICAL?

If you're doubting, Jesus is reaching out to you.

CRAIG GROESCHEL

B*e careful what you wish for—you might get it.* You've probably heard this old adage, or at least some version of it. It's a warning and a hopeful possibility all rolled into one.

Jonathan Malesic realized this truth after he attained his dream job but found it only ignited a power keg of disappointment and depression in his life. "My dream of being a college professor, which had sustained me through grad school, the job market, and the slow climb to tenure, has fallen apart," he explained in his book *The End of Burnout.*[1]

While Malesic focuses on burnout in work and career in his book, he finds similar dynamics at play in the church. Based on Malesic's definition of *burnout*—"the experience of being pulled between expectations and reality"— people don't leave the church because they're exhausted from doing too much. Rather, they leave because of the gap between their expectations of what the church *should* provide for them and what it *actually* provides.[2] As long as expectations and experiences are *aligned*, people can move forward.

In recent years, thousands of believers have experienced this kind of disconnect between the significance they hoped to find in Christian service and the frustration, loneliness, hypocrisy, and disappointment that actually represented their church experience. Simply put, they expected too much and got too little—so they quit trying. According to Malesic, when people experience such incongruity between their faith ideals and their life experience, the pressure builds until they abandon their ideals and resign themselves to reality elsewhere.

Although Malesic deems this a form of burnout, you might have heard it described in recent years by another term: *deconstruction*. This word has become a kind of catch-all for the experience of reconsidering, reflecting on, and even rejecting aspects of one's beliefs and practices along with churches, religious institutions, and ministries. Whether we call it *burnout* or *deconstruction*, the catalyst for this change is often the same—*doubt*.

◆ Based on your life experience, how would you define *burnout*? How does your definition describe where you've been, or where you are, in your faith journey?

◆ On a scale of 1 to 10, with 1 being "miles apart" and 10 being "almost perfectly aligned," what score best reflects the distance you've experienced between your ideals for your church experience and your actual reality? Why this number?

| 1 | 2 | 3 | 4 | 5 | 6 | 7 | 8 | 9 | 10 |

◆ What parallels do you see between burnout with your job and burnout with your faith? How are they distinctly different?

◆ How familiar are you with the term *deconstruction* as applied to someone's faith beliefs? How would you define it differently than burnout?

EXPLORING THE TRUTH

When you consider the basis for your Christian faith, you might point to a particular experience or a discussion with another believer that led to your salvation. Maybe you read a book, heard a sermon, or participated in a Bible study that had a profound impact on your understanding of Jesus and desire to follow him. Although narrowing your focus to one of these makes sense, the reality is that your faith was constructed over time by a variety of inputs.

If you consider your faith to be like a house, you've taken building materials from everything you've heard, seen, thought, felt, experienced, and discussed up to this point in your life to construct your overall understanding of God and the Christian life. Looking through the windows of your faith house, you view the world as best you can through God's eyes rather than human sight. Perhaps, when you consider the foundation of the faith house you've built, you feel pretty good about it. You are like the person Jesus described when he said, "Everyone who hears these words of mine and puts them into practice is like a wise man who built his house on the rock. The rain came down, the streams rose, and the winds blew and beat against that house; yet it did not fall, because it had its foundation on the rock" (Matthew 7:24–25).

We all want the security that comes from having the foundation of our faith built on the rock. We don't want to be like the other builder whom Jesus went on to describe: "But everyone who hears these words of mine and does not put them into practice is like a foolish man who built his house on sand. The rain came down, the streams rose, and the winds blew and beat against that house, and it fell with a great crash" (verses 26–27).

While the storms of life often emerge out of painful circumstances, unexpected losses, and bitter disappointments, your faith house can also get battered in more subtle ways. Consider how the harsh elements described by Jesus might represent your doubts, questions, and times of uncertainty. Instead of being leveled all at once by a hurricane event, your faith house might collapse after years of slow erosion in its foundation.

This brings us back to considering the building materials that have formed your faith. Jesus compared the strength of your foundation to how you respond to hearing his words and putting them into practice. We will come back to this crucial element later in this lesson, but first it's important to identify the other key materials that comprise your faith. Just as your doubts have a basis, which we explored in the previous lesson, so your beliefs about God, Jesus, and the Christian life have a basis that is worth examining as well.

◆ What seminal event, experience, conversation, or relationship comes to mind when you consider the basis for your Christian faith? What impact does this major contributor to your faith continue to exert in your life?

◆ Using your favorite terms about home-building styles, how would you describe your faith house? For example, does it seem more like a cabin in the woods, a midcentury modern cottage, or a split-level ranch style? Explain your response.

◆ Consider the following components that have contributed to your present faith house. Categorize them, along with a brief description, in the spaces below:

PERSONAL EXPERIENCES

1. _____
2. _____
3. _____

BIG EVENTS

4. _____
5. _____
6. _____

RELATIONSHIPS AND KEY CONVERSATIONS

7. _____
8. _____
9. _____

CHURCHES, MINISTRIES, ORGANIZATIONS

10. _____
11. _____
12. _____

◆ Look over your answers and circle the ones that have had the most positive impact on your faith. Underline the ones that you now consider questionable, harmful, or uncertain in their impact. How would you now assess the strength of your faith house with these various contributors in mind?

QUESTIONING THE TRUTH

No matter how strong your faith house may seem, you're probably aware of some cracks in the foundation. Perhaps certain family members instilled beliefs in you at a young age that you now see are not true. Or you had conversations with other believers that led you to accept certain subjective assumptions as biblical truth. Or maybe you've experienced trauma in your life that has forced you to reconsider why God allows suffering. You might recall the emotional high you felt at moments in your life during certain events, services, or retreats that have now faded—along with your heartfelt convictions at the time.

Don't worry if these cracks have shown up in your life. You're a human being, just like everyone else, and we all have some of these weak spots in our faith. The important thing now is how you will *respond* to these cracks. Think about this again in terms of a house. If a home has a weak foundation or rotten beams, those will need to be removed and/or restored in order for the house to be structurally sound. In the same way, the cracks and rotten beams in your faith house will need to be deconstructed in order for your faith to be structurally sound.

You might have heard certain definitions of deconstructing your faith, but here's a way to look at it based on how Jesus treated people. Deconstruction is simply *a spiritual journey in which you examine your faith in order to release and remove what is contrary to God's heart and embrace what is true*. Deconstruction can be beneficial in helping you understand what you believe and why you believe it. But it can also be destructive if you're not willing to separate the truth from the falsehoods. There's a better path than simply tearing down your beliefs and leaving your faith in ground-level ruins. Deconstruction prepares you for *reconstruction*.

In the Gospels, we often find Jesus challenging the traditional beliefs, practices, and assumptions that people held. Jesus knew that for his listeners to accept the truth of his message, they would have to examine their present set of beliefs. We see this particularly in the opening to the Sermon on the Mount in Matthew 5, where Jesus often begins by saying, "You have heard that it was said," before going on to turn people's expectations upside down with the truth of his gospel. Jesus used this contrast *five times* to deconstruct his listeners' old way of thinking (see verses 21, 27, 33, 38, 43). His example reminds us that it is not only *okay* to dislodge incorrect beliefs but also necessary to do so if we want to build a house of faith that has Christ as our foundation.

◆ What cracks have you experienced in your faith foundation? Which one has probably troubled you the most or caused the most doubt about certain beliefs?

◆ Which of these cracks in your faith do you now recognize has happened because a particular belief was not based on the truth of God's Word? Who or what helped instill that false assumption or faulty belief in your faith perspective?

◆ Read through Matthew 5:21–48. What are the old beliefs Jesus references? What does he say is true instead? Use the columns below to help you see how they contrast.

"You have heard that it was said . . . "	"But I tell you . . ."
verses 21–22	
verses 27–28	
verses 31–32	
verses 33–34	
verses 38–39	

◆ In what ways has God helped you see the incorrect beliefs and false assumptions you have held about him? How has he revealed what is actually true?

DIGGING DEEPER INTO DOUBT

Rather than doubt being a wrecking ball that smashes everything, it can operate as one of those detectors used for measuring radon, carbon dioxide, or toxic mold. These devices indicate where the problems are so they can then be remediated. The troublesome areas might need to be torn out and rebuilt, but the solid, nontoxic parts of the structure remain intact.

If you're struggling to see doubt in a more positive light, just consider Peter, the disciple who may have doubted more than Thomas. One scene in particular in Matthew 14:13–33 illustrates the way Peter's faith could go from fantastically buoyant to fearfully weighted by doubt. Jesus, after miraculously feeding more than five thousand people, sent the disciples ahead by boat as he dismissed the crowd. He then spent some time in prayer before catching up to them shortly before dawn. Only, Jesus caught up to them by *walking on the water*.

The disciples were terrified and cried out that they must be seeing a ghost. But Jesus reassured them, saying, "It is I. Don't be afraid" (verse 27). Peter evidently wasn't convinced. In spite of the fact that he had just witnessed the miracle of Jesus feeding the five thousand, he was not prepared to witness the miracle of Jesus walking on the water. So, rather than waiting to see what would happen, Peter blurted out, "Lord, if it's you . . . tell me to come to you on the water." To this, Jesus responded, "Come" (verses 28–29).

We are not told how long it took for Peter to get out of the boat, but he eventually followed the Lord's instruction and "walked on the water and came toward Jesus" (verse 29). Peter had faith that if Jesus could walk on water, then he could empower him to do so as well. Yet his faith quickly hit a snag: "When he saw the wind, he was afraid and, beginning to sink, cried out, 'Lord, save me!' Immediately

Jesus reached out his hand and caught him. 'You of little faith,' he said, 'why did you doubt?'" (verses 30–31).

Perhaps the reality of what Peter was doing suddenly registered with him. When he saw the wind whipping up the water's surface, his doubts distracted him. Peter became afraid, began to sink, and cried for Jesus to save him. Notice the sequence of what happened next: (1) Jesus "reached out his hand and caught him," and then (2) Jesus said, "You of little faith . . . why did you doubt?"

We might assume that Jesus was calling Peter out for allowing his doubts to pull him under. But in light of how quickly Jesus reached out to grab his disciple, this isn't necessarily the case. Instead of *tsk-tsk*ing Peter for having doubts, what if Jesus was inviting Peter to consider what had just happened and use it to strengthen his faith? What if Jesus was reminding Peter of what he knew to be true—almost as if saying, "Don't you remember who I am? Remember those times you've seen me do the impossible? Water into wine? Loaves and fishes to feed thousands? Restoring sight to the blind? You know me, Peter, or you wouldn't have gotten out of the boat. You had faith enough to walk on water. So keep believing!"

The next time you experience doubt, look for the hand of love to pull you up. View your doubt as Jesus' invitation to experience a deeper faith.

◆ When has your doubt felt more like a wrecking ball than a problem detector? Why were you tempted to stop with deconstruction rather than assess how to rebuild your faith?

◆ What stands out for you in the scene with Jesus and Peter walking on the water? Why do you think it resonates so strongly with you?

◆ When have you experienced spiritual growth only to sink suddenly when something caused you to doubt? What did you learn from that situation?

◆ How will reconsidering doubt as an invitation to a deeper faith change the way you deconstruct your beliefs? What areas of your faith still need to be addressed based on the doubts that you have?

DOUBTFUL AT BEST

When you consider doubt as an invitation to a deeper faith, you realize you don't have to be afraid of deconstructing what you believe. You know it's healthy and necessary to release what has been holding you back so you can grasp the gifts of truth that God offers. However, moving from the deconstruction phase to the reconstruction phase still takes time.

Discernment and *timing* are crucial when it comes to allowing doubt to help you reconstruct a stronger faith. As Solomon, the wisest man who ever lived, reminds us, there is "a time to tear down and a time to build" (Ecclesiastes 3:3). If you've watched home-renovation shows on TV, you know that it's easy enough to grab a sledgehammer or fire up a bulldozer to demolish the old structure. But rebuilding and renovating the remaining parts into something new and stronger takes considerable time and effort.

Deconstruction requires thoughtful reflection, sincere questioning, and an openness to what may be uncomfortable. As you deconstruct, ask if you're questioning what you believed with reckless abandon or with careful curiosity. Are you genuinely looking for what's true so you can build from it? Or are you just looking to knock down your entire belief system?

As you begin reconstructing, also consider the source for your new building materials. There are countless people, churches, denominations, ministries, and organizations eager to offer you their options. How do you decide who you listen to and rely on as a source of truth? The answer is *none of them*! Remember, it was the opinions of others that likely contributed to your shaky foundation in the first place. Instead, look at Jesus. He said that if you listen to his words and put them into practice, your foundation will be built on the rock. He is your picture of God: "Anyone who has seen me has seen the Father!" (John 14:9 NLT).

Your understanding of what is true about God should be centered solely on Christ. The Bible provides a very detailed picture of Jesus, which allows you to develop an accurate picture of God. Knowing that God looks like Jesus can help you sort through the clutter and confusion of deconstruction and rebuild a bedrock faith foundation.

The life of Jesus is your example. When you look at his life, you find that he was exceptional in his character, his love, and his compassion. He consistently cared for those who were hurting, welcomed the outcasts, and cried with his friends. He treated people with grace and tenderness—even the prostitutes, tax collectors, and adulterers. He saw the best in the worst of sinners and reached out to the lonely, the lost, and the least in society.

This is who God is, and you can trust him—no matter what life brings.

◆ What concerns do you have about shifting from deconstructing your beliefs to reconstructing a stronger faith? What excites you most about this shift?

◆ When have you used past doubts as a license to stop believing altogether and move away from anything to do with God? What has drawn you back to rebuilding your faith rather than simply settling for complete deconstruction?

◆ What questions, thoughts, and feelings stir inside you when you consider relying solely on Jesus as your source for what is true? What is challenging about focusing only on Jesus and his example as your faith foundation?

◆ How would you describe the way Jesus viewed doubt, based on the passages and examples you have read so far? How has your understanding of the way Jesus regarded doubt changed since you began this study?

NOTES

1. Jonathan Malesic, *The End of Burnout*, (Oakland, CA: University of California Press, 2022), 8.
2. Malesic, *The End of Burnout*, 9.

PART 2

OUR DOUBTS

It's one thing to doubt aspects of your faith as a way to strengthen your faith. But drilling into specific questions, often rooted in personal pain, will take your doubt to the next level. Asking the hard questions head-on can be disturbing, disruptive, and discouraging if you simply use them as weapons of mass deconstruction. If, though, your intent is to assess your faith in order to reconstruct it more accurately, more honestly, and more powerfully, then asking questions with integrity will be a step toward healing. Here are the key principles you will learn in part 2:

- You're not alone in questioning the basics of faith, including God's character, free will, prayer, judgment, hell, the Bible versus science, and divine love.
- The hard questions that emerge out of doubt are expressed, described, and often illustrated by people in the Bible.
- God never tells you not to ask questions—but he does tell you to be prepared not to like the answers or to not get an answer.
- Tackling doubt's big questions requires courage, patience, and openness to new ways of considering what they reveal—about you and God.
- Ultimately, the hard questions contributing to doubt become personal—not theoretical, theological, or philosophical—which provides a more relevant motivation for exploring them honestly.

WHY SHOULD I BELIEVE GOD IS GOOD?

*With God's love we have to remember the presence of pain
does not indicate an absence of love. In fact, oftentimes,
the presence of real pain is the evidence of real love.*

CRAIG GROESCHEL

If you frequent drive-throughs, you may have experienced the surprise of having the driver in the car ahead of you pay for your order. Perhaps this act of generosity even inspired you to do the same and pay for the meal of the person behind you. This everyday method of "paying it forward" occurs frequently in societies today.

Maybe you've practiced such random acts of kindness in other ways, such as through giving money to support the ministries of your church or another nonprofit organization—and not just to get the tax benefits of charitable giving! Or perhaps your act of kindness was more hands-on, such as through volunteering at shelters and food banks or mentoring at-risk students. Or maybe you like to be more spontaneous in your serving and meet needs as you encounter them, whether giving cash to someone requesting help near a busy intersection or paying for the meal of a young family at a restaurant.

There are countless ways for you to show kindness to people—and for them to show kindness to you. Yet the truth is that people often demonstrate the opposite. Crime, violence, prejudice, division, and the like are prevalent in our society today. This has caused many to doubt that God is as good as the Bible declares him to be. After all, the argument goes, if he really is such a good God, then why does he allow all the pain and suffering we find in our world today?

◆ When has someone recently surprised you with a random act of kindness? How did you respond during that experience?

◆ When have you recently done a good deed for someone else unexpectedly? What prompted you to do that act of kindness?

◆ How do you view the impact that such acts of kindness can have on others? Does showing others kindness prevent or impede human selfishness?

◆ What is your primary motivation when you give money, time, attention, and other resources to people in need? How would you describe the pattern of your giving—sporadic, frequent, consistent, anonymous, or something else?

EXPLORING THE TRUTH

You might agree at an intellectual level that God is, by definition, inherently good. Yet your understanding of his goodness may have taken a few hits in light of the losses, tragedies, and disappointments that you've experienced in this life. Christians are often quick to proclaim, "God is good—all the time," yet his goodness can be hard to spot in the midst of losing a loved one to cancer or experiencing a betrayal from a once-trusted ally.

Sometimes, your doubts will multiply when you feel you've been faithfully serving God and following his call on your life, but you're still struggling with a loss of income or other trial. Even looking beyond yourself, it can be hard to fathom how a good God would allow all the suffering we see. How can God be *good*—all the time—when there is so much pain and outright *evil* in the world?

More than two thousand years ago, the Greek philosopher Epicurus presented a three-point argument refuting the goodness of God. Epicurus reasoned that if God could not prevent evil and its impact in our lives, then he obviously was not all-powerful. On the other hand, if God could prevent evil and was not willing to do so, then he could not be good. And if God was both willing and able to prevent evil, then why does evil exist? Making such statements actually requires considering more options than Epicurus included. Is it possible that Christianity could give meaning to the existence of good and evil and offer a solution for the evil and suffering that we experience?

While we are often conditioned to view the Bible as the source of answers, it is also filled with questions—the same kind of hard questions that doubt forces us to ask. Instead of ignoring thorny questions that reflect our doubts, the Bible includes numerous stories of uncertainty, loss, violence, confusion, suffering, and pain.

One of the most prolific questioners in the Bible was David, the renowned shepherd-king of Israel whom God described as a man after his own heart (see 1 Samuel 13:14). David consistently trusted the Lord, but he also questioned God, as we frequently see in the many psalms that he wrote. Although many of these offer poetic prayers and praise songs, almost as many directly question God—with the same questions we wrestle with today.

> [1] *My God, my God, why have you forsaken me?*
> *Why are you so far from saving me,*
> *so far from my cries of anguish?*
> [2] *My God, I cry out by day, but you do not answer,*
> *by night, but I find no rest.*
>
> [3] *Yet you are enthroned as the Holy One;*
> *you are the one Israel praises.*
> [4] *In you our ancestors put their trust;*
> *they trusted and you delivered them.*
> [5] *To you they cried out and were saved;*
> *in you they trusted and were not put to shame.*
>
> [6] *But I am a worm and not a man,*
> *scorned by everyone, despised by the people.*
> [7] *All who see me mock me;*
> *they hurl insults, shaking their heads.*
> [8] *"He trusts in the LORD," they say,*
> *"let the LORD rescue him.*
> *Let him deliver him,*
> *since he delights in him."*

> [9] *Yet you brought me out of the womb;*
>   *you made me trust in you, even at my mother's breast.*
> [10] *From birth I was cast on you;*
>   *from my mother's womb you have been my God.*
> [11] *Do not be far from me,*
>   *for trouble is near*
>   *and there is no one to help.*

PSALM 22:1-11

◆ How have you handled your life's greatest losses and toughest challenges? When has one of these caused you to doubt the goodness of God?

◆ What have you been taught about how to consider the problem of evil? What assumptions have you reached about why God allows hard things to happen?

◆ What stands out to you the most in this first half of Psalm 22? What difference does knowing it was written by David make for you? Why?

◆ When have you felt like a "worm" and not a person? What was the context for that situation when you felt that low?

QUESTIONING THE TRUTH

David wasn't the only one to question God in the Bible. The prophet Jeremiah wrote the Old Testament book called Lamentations, which is basically a big prayer-poem of sadness. While this makes sense given that a *lament* is a poem or song of sorrow, the original translation of the name of the book was "How?" As in, "How could you allow this, God? How could you not stop our sadness and suffering? How long will this last?" Jeremiah's testimony certainly challenges the goodness of God: "I am the man who has seen affliction by the rod of the LORD's wrath. He has driven me away and made me walk in darkness rather than light; indeed, he has turned his hand against me again and again, all day long" (Lamentations 3:1–3).

Then there's the prophet Elijah, who spiraled into depression and hid in a cave after engineering one of God's most dramatic displays of power—igniting a water-soaked stone altar. There's also Ruth's mother-in-law, Naomi, who wanted to change her name to Mara, meaning "bitter," after losing her husband and two sons. And even the wisest king of Israel, David's son Solomon, who experienced wealth, luxury, and virtually every pleasure known, still struggled with doubt, as chronicled in the Old Testament book of Ecclesiastes.

In the New Testament, we find John the Baptist, the cousin of Jesus, whose purpose was to prepare the way for the Messiah. Surely, if anyone deserved divine intervention in the face of danger, it was John. After all, he had fulfilled God's call, even baptizing Jesus in the Jordan River at the start of his ministry. Instead, John was wrongly arrested and put in prison. Surely, Jesus could have rescued him in the blink of an eye. But he didn't . . . and John was beheaded.

Even those who triumphed and became inspiring heroes of the faith were not exempt from pain and suffering. In Hebrews 11, known as the Faith Hall of Fame, we find a gruesome catalog of the various ways God's faithful followers suffered: "Some faced jeers and flogging, and even chains and imprisonment. They were put to death by stoning; they were sawed in two; they were killed by the sword. They went about in sheepskins and goatskins, destitute, persecuted and mistreated—the world was not worthy of them. They wandered in deserts and mountains, living in caves and in holes in the ground" (verses 36–38).

Even Jesus, the Son of God—though a conquering and victorious king—is called "a Man of sorrows and acquainted with grief" (Isaiah 53:3 NKJV). And if the opening of Psalm 22 sounds familiar, it may be because you recall Jesus uttering its opening question while dying on the cross: "My God, my God, why have you forsaken me?" (Matthew 27:46).

Why include so many examples of questioning God's goodness in the very book the Holy Spirit inspired? Why would God show us so many of his chosen ones who complained about him and his goodness? Perhaps because God wants to show us that he can be loving *and* allow suffering at the same time.

◆ Which of the doubters and questioners in the Bible stand out to you? How do you identify with them and the way they questioned God's goodness?

◆ How do you respond to the idea that God is good and loving but still allows us to suffer? Why does he not prevent us from experiencing life's trauma?

◆ What feelings rise up within you as you consider that loving and serving God does *not* prevent you from experiencing danger, pain, and suffering?

◆ When have you found yourself in a situation where you needed to cause discomfort to others for their own good (such disciplining a child)? How did you handle this tension?

DIGGING DEEPER INTO DOUBT

How is it possible that God is good and loving yet still allows suffering? More importantly, how is it possible that God allows suffering because he *is* loving and good? Answering those questions requires us to reconsider how we define *love* and contemplate it from God's perspective. We tend to define *love* as an emotion, but Scripture teaches that God is love (see 1 John 4:16). Love isn't just what God feels or does—love is who God is. The Bible tells us that not only is God the essence of love, but also that he created us for love—to love and be loved by him, and to love others and be loved by them (see Matthew 22:37–39).

Now, in order for love to be love, it must be freely chosen. Being forced or coerced to love someone simply doesn't work—it does not represent real love. God, at his core, is love and made us for love, which necessitated his creating us with free will and giving us the power to choose. By giving us this freedom to choose whether or not we will love him and other people, we are also forced to live with the consequences—we also have the freedom to choose *not* to love and to choose hate instead. If we're given the freedom to choose what's good and right, then we also face the option of choosing what's evil and wrong.

This freedom to choose, as we witness in the story of Adam and Eve in the Bible, resulted in humans making choices that didn't align with God's love. Simply put, the gift of free choice brought sin into the world when Adam and Eve chose to disobey God. Ever since, humans have continued to use their freedom to choose selfishness rather than loving the way God loves. Ultimately, it's human sin that results in the evil and suffering in the world.

If God were to remove evil and suffering, he would also have to remove our freedom to choose—and thereby remove love. And without God's love as our standard of authority for what is good and evil, we would be left to our own individual human opinions. We would have no *objective standard* for right and wrong.

So, the presence of evil and suffering doesn't prove that God is absent or indifferent to our pain. Ironically, it actually proves that God *does* exist. The fact that we experience grief, pain, betrayal, and tragic loss is not evidence of love's absence—it is evidence that it exists.

◆ How do you explain the difference between the way most people define *love* and the way God defines it? What does it mean to you that "God is love"?

◆ How did God's gift of free will introduce the problem of sin into this world? How do the sinful choices that human beings make today result in evil and suffering?

◆ How does the presence of pain in your life provide evidence for God's love? How does understanding the way God's love necessitates free will change the way you consider suffering in your life?

◆ When have you experienced "tough love" from someone you trusted and knew wanted what was best for you? When have you exercised tough love in order to care for someone in spite of knowing how it would affect them temporarily?

DOUBTFUL AT BEST

You may regard yourself as a good person and know others whom you also regard as good people. Unfortunately, no one is good enough by God's standard. "All have sinned and fall short of the glory of God" (Romans 3:23) and "there is no one righteous, not even one" (verse 10). Without the transforming work of Christ, *no one* has a good heart.

Jesus once encountered a man who was wrestling with the question of what it means to be good, and their conversation reveals the answer to the question of God's goodness. Jesus was on his way to Jerusalem when this man came running up to him, fell down on his knees, and asked, "Good Teacher, what must I do to inherit eternal life?"

"Why do you call me good?" Jesus asked. "Only God is truly good" (Mark 10:17–18 NLT). Their discussion then turned to keeping God's law—which the man said he had done. Then the conversation shifted to the heart of the matter: "Looking at the man, Jesus felt genuine love for him. 'There is still one thing you haven't done,' he told him. 'Go and sell all your possessions and give the money to the poor, and you will have treasure in heaven. Then come, follow me.' At this the man's face fell, and he went away sad, for he had many possessions" (verses 21–22 NLT).

No matter how well-intended we might be, none of us are good enough to match God's love. There has been only one truly good person in history: Jesus. He, the only good and perfect person to ever live, never did anything wrong. He, the sinless Son of God, gave up the glory of heaven and was born into poverty as a baby in a manger. Later, when his ministry got off the ground, his family thought he had lost his mind. After almost three years together, his closest friends abandoned him—and one even betrayed him. Jesus was falsely accused, wrongly imprisoned, tortured, stripped, mocked, and shamefully crucified. The only one who was good—who had never sinned—became sin for us. He was temporarily separated from his heavenly Father so we wouldn't have to be eternally separated from our heavenly Father. Jesus made the choice to give up his life so he could give us new life.

And God allowed his Son to go through that pain because he loves you so much! "For God so loved the world that he gave his one and only Son" (John 3:16). He loves you so much that he sent Jesus to die for you—not because you're good, but just because he loves you.

◆ Who is someone you consider to be a "good person"? What is the basis for their goodness?

◆ Why are we incapable of achieving God's level of perfect love and goodness? How did God resolve this incapacity by sending Jesus to die on the cross?

◆ What frustrates you the most about this lesson and its exploration of God's goodness? What questions and concerns continue to linger?

◆ Read Psalms 10, 22, and 77, which all express the author's questions toward God. Then write your own psalm expressing the questions you have for God right now. Your psalm might be all questions and no answers. As long as it's sincere, don't worry about the form or "right way" to craft it. Simply allow it to express the questions of your heart concerning God's love and goodness.

WHY DOESN'T GOD ANSWER MY PRAYERS?

The purpose of prayer is not to get God to do our will.
The purpose of prayer is to know God so we can do his will.

CRAIG GROESCHEL

"Unanswered prayers" are more than just the title of a country song from the 1990s. They are an inevitable part of our journey of faith and will often force us to reconsider how we relate and communicate with God. When our most important prayers go unanswered, seemingly ignored by God, we feel angry, abandoned, hurt, and disappointed—all these feelings swirling in a vortex of doubt. We might also be reluctant to share our doubts and accompanying feelings with others out of concern for how they might view us and our faith.

One iconic twentieth-century Christian knew exactly how this feels. In one of his books, he expressed his doubts resulting from unanswered prayer with such raw emotion and candor that he decided to publish it under a pseudonym: N. W. Clerk. Apparently, this British theologian feared the way his honest doubts might undermine his many other books, lectures, and articles on the Christian faith—and how his readers might change their opinion of him.[1]

He had married late in life. Initially, this was just for friendship and companionship—basically, a favor to his new expatriate wife so she and her children could remain in Britain. But then she became ill with bone cancer, and the two of them realized how their bond had become love. Despite enjoying a brief time of remission, she died four years after marrying this scholar, theologian, and writer—whom the world knows as C. S. Lewis. And the book he published under the pen name remains one of his most powerful works: *A Grief Observed*.[2]

Within its pages, Lewis described how his desperate prayers for his wife to be healed went unheeded. He felt that the more fervently he prayed, the more deafening God's silence was: "When you are happy . . . and turn to Him with gratitude and praise, you will be—or so it feels—welcomed with open arms. But go to Him when your need is desperate, when all other help is vain, and what do you find? A door slammed in your face."[3]

The book Lewis feared would undermine the testimony of his Christian faith now gives countless readers permission to doubt—and to seek God in the midst of their doubting. Lewis persevered and realized that as he grieved, he had "gradually been coming to feel that the door is no longer shut and bolted."[4] Rather than continuing to view God's silence as abandonment, he saw how God was using it to strengthen his faith and draw him into a more intimate relationship. His loss wasn't any less painful, but his willingness to question why God didn't answer his prayers became an unexpected opportunity for a richer faith.

◆ How would you describe your prayer life over the past year? What and who has influenced the way you incorporate prayer into your life?

◆ What frustrations and disappointments have you experienced when you pray? What aspects of prayer have you enjoyed the most?

◆ What is one request you continue to make that has gone unanswered for a long time? What thoughts and feelings accompany this unanswered prayer request?

◆ When C. S. Lewis's prayers for his wife's healing went unanswered, he compared the experience to having a door slammed in his face. What analogy would you use to describe your experience with unanswered prayer?

EXPLORING THE TRUTH

If you've read much of the Bible, you know there is power in prayer. Actually, considering some of the amazing ways that God answered seemingly impossible prayers, it's hard *not* to notice.

For instance, there's the time when Joshua prayed for the sun to stand still, and it did—for an entire day (see Joshua 10:12–14). Or when Elijah faced off against the followers of Baal and prayed for a sacrifice to catch fire spontaneously on the altar. Just to leave no room for doubt, Elijah soaked the altar with gallons of water repeatedly (see 1 Kings 18:22–40). And did fire rain down from heaven and torch that altar? You bet it did! And don't forget about Daniel, who continued to pray after the Persian king made it illegal on threat of death. Daniel ended up in a den of hungry lions . . . which we can only assume really made him pray! God answered by shutting the mouths of those lions and sparing Daniel's life (see Daniel 6:6–23).

Clearly, God answers prayers. You've likely seen him answer many of your own prayers. They may not be as jaw-dropping as the ones found in the Bible—or, then again, they may rival them because you experienced them firsthand. Yet you've inevitably also experienced situations where you prayed for God's help—urgently and desperately—only to find that your prayers seemed to go unanswered.

Jesus made the promise, "I will do whatever you ask in my name, so that the Father may be glorified in the Son. You may ask me for anything in my name, and I will do it" (John 14:13–14). And yet, based on our own experiences, prayer is a mixed bag. Prayer is powerful, and also confusing. It can be dynamic, and also disappointing. God answers prayers, and yet sometimes he doesn't. Prayer leads to blessings, but can also lead to bitterness. It makes us wonder where the problem lies—whether we're praying the "right" way or whether God really cares about our requests.

Paul understood the challenge of having a prayer go unanswered. And not just any prayer, but one that was evidently quite personal to him. It was something that troubled him so much he asked God *three times* to address the problem.

Coming from Paul, you'd think God wouldn't hesitate to answer his prayer. After all, this is the same Paul whose life dramatically changed after encountering Christ on the road to Damascus. It's the same Paul who preached the gospel for three decades while wandering from place to place around the Mediterranean. The Paul who served Jesus so faithfully that he was persecuted, beaten, stoned, and imprisoned. The same Paul whom God used to heal diseases, cast out demons, and raise the dead. The Paul who wrote a quarter of the New Testament. Yet this Paul, just like everyone else, had to wrestle with unanswered prayers.

> *7 Therefore, in order to keep me from becoming conceited, I was given a thorn in my flesh, a messenger of Satan, to torment me. 8 Three times I pleaded with the Lord to take it away from me. 9 But he said to me, "My grace is sufficient for you, for my power is made perfect in weakness." Therefore I will boast all*

the more gladly about my weaknesses, so that Christ's power may rest on me.
¹⁰ That is why, for Christ's sake, I delight in weaknesses, in insults, in hardships,
in persecutions, in difficulties. For when I am weak, then I am strong.

2 CORINTHIANS 12:7–10

◆ What is one of your favorite examples of an answered prayer in the Bible?
Why does it stand out to you?

◆ When has God answered one of your prayers in a dramatic or unexpected
way? What did you learn about the power of prayer from that experience?

◆ What frustrates you when it comes to prayer? How does that affect the way
you pray?

◆ What conclusions did Paul reach for why God did not answer his requests
to remove the thorn in his flesh? How do you respond to Paul's conclusions?

QUESTIONING THE TRUTH

Sometimes when our prayers go unanswered, we may wonder if we are the problem. The fact is, based on what Jesus said, we just might be. When Jesus was talking to his disciples about the relationship between faith and prayer, he said that if they had faith in God, they could move mountains. He continued with this remark: "Therefore I tell you, whatever you ask for in prayer, believe that you have received it, and it will be yours" (Mark 11:24).

Before you assume this is just another big promise that is not true in your experience, consider what Jesus said next: "And when you stand praying, if you hold anything against anyone, forgive them, so that your Father in heaven may forgive you your sins" (verse 25). Jesus said something similar regarding the state of our heart when we make an offering: "If you are offering your gift at the altar and there remember that your brother or sister has something against you, leave your gift there in front of the altar. First go and be reconciled to them; then come and offer your gift" (Matthew 5:23-24). In other words, don't offer God something when you should be offering to make amends with someone you've offended.

Clearly, the state of our relationships with other people matters when we pray. Jesus instructed us to make sure our relational accounts are in order before we pray or make an offering. He emphasized the need for us to prioritize the type of people we're becoming rather than asking God for anything or thinking we're ready to offer what we have to others.

Perhaps you've found it difficult at times to pray when you know you've sinned against another person. In fact, if you consider a time when your prayers went unanswered, you might find that this was the case. Think about what the attitude of your heart was in that moment—particularly toward other people. Did you have an outstanding relational conflict that needed to be addressed? Perhaps God wanted you to seek that relational healing before you continued asking for that particular request. Sometimes, this will be the source of the problem.

◆ Why do you think God wants your relationships to be in good standing before you make your requests to him?

◆ When have you realized you needed to make amends with someone so you could continue to grow in your faith? How does being at odds with others affect the way you view God?

◆ When was the last time that you asked someone to forgive you in order to mend the relationship? Which of your relationships are currently in need of this kind of healing?

◆ Who do you need to contact to schedule a time to get together and clear the air? Write down their name and when you plan to meet. What is the most important thing you need to tell that person?

DIGGING DEEPER INTO DOUBT

When it comes to unanswered prayers, we also need to check our motives. Sure, it's tough to ever have *completely* selfless motives, but often our prayers are motivated solely by our ego. Some of us might pray to win the lottery, for instance, but it might be better for us to check our motives and take a look at how we're currently stewarding all God has entrusted to us.

Once again, though, we're not alone in having selfish motives. In Jesus' time, the Pharisees were more concerned about sounding pious in their prayers than actually praying with an open heart to God. They usually prayed in public, often on street corners and outside the temple where everyone would notice them. They wore fancy robes that signified their religious status and prayed eloquent prayers that they thought would impress everyone.

But nothing about the way they prayed impressed Jesus. He repeatedly called them out for their hypocrisy, pretense, and self-righteousness. "Everything they do is done for people to see," he said (Matthew 23:5). Jesus compared them to dishes that get washed on the outside but are left dirty on the inside and elaborate tombs that have beautiful exteriors but nasty interiors filled with death and decay. He concluded, "On the outside you appear to people as righteous but on the inside you are full of hypocrisy and wickedness" (verse 28).

You may not put on a show when you pray like the Pharisees, but that doesn't mean your motives are always pure. James addressed this directly when he wrote, "You do not have because you do not ask God. When you ask, you do not receive, because you ask with wrong motives, that you may spend what you get on your pleasures" (4:2–3).

Could it be that God doesn't give you what you want because he knows it will keep you from recognizing what you really need—*him*? Perhaps God doesn't answer a prayer when it's a selfish request because he is trying to help you think less about yourself and more about others. Perhaps he hasn't answered a prayer because he wants to increase your faith.

Having faith really matters to God. Not only is faith what makes you right before him, but also, "without faith it is impossible to please God" (Hebrews 11:6). Jesus once had two blind men call out to him for healing, and he asked them, "Do you believe that I am able to do this?" When they answered yes, Jesus touched their eyes and said, "According to your faith let it be done to you," and they were healed (Matthew 9:28–30). When Jesus healed a woman who had endured a serious illness for twelve years, he said to her, "Your faith has healed you" (Mark 5:34). Other examples make it similarly clear that *your faith matters to God.*

◆ How do you feel about praying aloud in front of others? Do you pray differently when you know others are listening versus when you pray silently or alone?

◆ What is a prayer request you've made that you now recognize was based on selfish motives? What prevented you from seeing your motives at the time?

◆ What do you think it means to have faith when you pray? Why do you think having faith for what you request is impacted by your motives?

◆ When has God answered one of your prayers in a powerful or even miraculous way? How does this experience impact your level of faith when you pray now?

DOUBTFUL AT BEST

Despite how you may feel at times, you can be confident that God hears you and cares about you. As John wrote, "This is the confidence we have in approaching God: that if we ask anything according to his will, he hears us. And if we know that he hears us—whatever we ask—we know that we have what we asked of him" (1 John 5:14–15). God is not ignoring you during those times when you're not getting an answer to certain prayers. He might just have something better in mind. This something better is what we refer to as "God's will."

You're probably familiar with the best-known prayer in the Bible, usually called the Lord's Prayer. It is the template that Jesus gave his followers when they noticed that he didn't pray like everyone else. Jesus' prayers were relational and addressed a loving heavenly Father. They expressed a profound trust in God for provision, protection, and ongoing advancement of his kingdom. The Lord's Prayer remains a model for how we can communicate with God today:

> [9] *"This, then, is how you should pray:*
>
> > *'Our Father in heaven,*
> > *hallowed be your name,*
> > [10] *your kingdom come,*
> > *your will be done,*
> > > *on earth as it is in heaven.*
> > [11] *Give us today our daily bread.*
> > [12] *And forgive us our debts,*
> > > *as we also have forgiven our debtors.*
> > [13] *And lead us not into temptation,*
> > > *but deliver us from the evil one.'"*

MATTHEW 6:9–13

This model of prayer reveals how you can exercise faith while keeping your motives in check. It reminds you that prayer isn't about getting things from God, which ultimately becomes transactional, but is more sacred, beautiful, and intimate than any kind of transaction. When you pray, you're communicating with a God who knows you, loves you more than you can imagine, and is inviting you to partner with him in his mission.

Prayer isn't about trying to control God; it's about giving him control. The purpose of prayer is not about getting God to do *your* will. It's about knowing God so you can do *his* will.

◆ What does it mean for you to pray that "God's will" be done? What concerns, fears, or questions arise when you pray for his will to be done in your life?

◆ How does praying consistently help align you with God's will? What aspects of prayer require you to focus more on others and God and less on yourself?

◆ What stands out when you consider the Lord's Prayer as a model for how you should pray? How does it address your questions and concerns about God not always answering your prayers?

◆ Based on your understanding of prayer, how do you presently pray the Lord's Prayer? Rewrite it below in your own words, avoiding the familiar language you may have memorized as much as possible.

NOTES

1. C. S. Lewis, *A Grief Observed* (London: Faber & Faber, 1964), publisher's note on dust jacket.
2. Lewis, *A Grief Observed,* publisher's note on dust jacket.
3. Lewis, *A Grief Observed,* 5.
4. Lewis, *A Grief Observed,* 46.

WHY WOULD GOD ONLY PROVIDE ONE WAY?

God provided one way in Jesus. Christians believe
that not out of arrogance but from evidence.

CRAIG GROESCHEL

H ave you ever driven the wrong way down a one-way street? If so, you know the shock of looking up to see another vehicle headed straight toward you. The danger you fear in that moment is indeed life-threatening. According to recent studies by the National Transportation Safety Board, wrong-way driving (which is defined as operating a vehicle in a direction against the intended flow of traffic) results in some of the most severe types of crashes.[1]

In a comprehensive study done by the Iowa State University Institute for Transportation, researchers concluded the problem of wrong-way driving isn't limited to urban areas with congested traffic patterns or higher concentrations of one-way streets. Rather, the researchers found that "wrong-way driving can occur on a variety of roadways including divided highways, freeways or arterial roads" often stemming from "driver confusion resulting from roadways that are challenging to navigate."[2] In other words, drivers are responsible for going the wrong way, but unmarked streets and unclear signage can contribute to their confusion.

If you've made this kind of error, the best-case scenario is that you realized your mistake and quickly made a U-turn. But imagine if you continued driving in the wrong direction because you didn't feel it was fair that you could only drive in one direction. You didn't believe your freedom to drive the way you want should be determined by some transportation authority. If you did this, others might soon follow your example, making one-way signs not only inaccurate but also irrelevant. Everyone would be free to drive however they wanted, regardless of rules, regulations, signs, and traffic laws.

In many ways, this illustration reflects the way that faith beliefs have evolved in our culture. People are encouraged to believe whatever they want and live out their own truth. God loves all people, the reasoning goes, so shouldn't we be inclusive of all faiths and get over all our hang-ups about there being only one way to God? It's an important question—and one that has an answer many people might not like. This is because sometimes, just like when driving down the road, there is only one way to reach the destination.

◆ How would you describe the experience of driving the wrong way down a one-way street? Or, if you have been fortunate enough *not* to experience this, what do you imagine it would be like?

◆ If a nonbelieving friend asked, "Why would God provide only one way to salvation?" how would you respond? How often do you consider this question?

◆ What other situations come to mind when you think of Jesus being the only way to salvation? How often do you encounter problems with only one solution?

◆ How would you explain the difference between being inclusive versus exclusive in our culture? How do you think most people make the distinction?

EXPLORING THE TRUTH

You might recall from your elementary school language classes that there's an important difference between the article *a* and the article *the*. Basically, using *a* refers to one of many, or one of a number of things that are similar. So, if you say *a* giraffe or *a* family or *a* piece of cake, you're leaving room for all the other giraffes, families, and pieces of cake out there.

However, if you use the article *the*, the assumption is that you're referencing just one thing, either because it's unique or because it's the only one you're talking about. So, for example, saying you're going to *a* restaurant could mean any number of restaurants, but saying you're going to *the* restaurant means you have a particular one in mind. In grammatical terms, *a* is an indefinite article while *the* is a definite article.

But who cares, right? Why the fourth-grade review on parts of speech? The reason is because precision with language matters, especially when the person speaking is Jesus. He declared, "I am the way and the truth and the life. No one comes to the Father except through me" (John 14:6). Notice he said *the* way and not *a* way. *The* way means there is no other way. If there were other ways, then perhaps Jesus would have said, "I am *a* way and *a* truth and *a* life. You might get to the Father through me, or you might get to him another way."

But Jesus didn't say that. The language is clear, whether in the original Greek or translated into English. Jesus said he is the *one* way, *one* truth, and *one* life. The only way to the Father is through him. Reinforcing his point, he left no room for exceptions—"no one" and "except through me."

Sounds rather narrow, doesn't it? It certainly flies in the face of our contemporary trend to include everyone in everything. Exclusivity today smacks of an elitism that elevates one person or group above another based on criteria that someone else decides. We are all human and equal in God's sight, right? So how can Jesus be the *only* way to know God?

Maybe you've heard it said there are many paths to God—that people of different faiths can coexist knowing they are all worshiping the same deity and will end up in the same place. Considering the vast number of people, communities, societies, and cultures that have flourished across all of time and history, it certainly seems logical that there would be many different ways to worship, live by faith, pray, and know God.

Yet Jesus said he is the way. *The* way. So where does that leave us when it comes to those who don't believe in Jesus? Before we explore that thorny question further, it's helpful to first consider some of the other bold "I am" statements that Jesus made. These statements can shed light on this whole idea of him being the only way. The Gospel of John is full of them:

"I am the bread of life. Whoever comes to me will never go hungry, and whoever believes in me will never be thirsty" (6:35).

"I am the light of the world. Whoever follows me will never walk in darkness, but will have the light of life" (8:12).

"I am the gate; whoever enters through me will be saved. They will come in and go out, and find pasture" (10:9).

"I am the good shepherd. The good shepherd lays down his life for the sheep" (10:11).

"I am the resurrection and the life. The one who believes in me will live, even though they die; and whoever lives by believing in me will never die" (11:25–26).

"I am the way and the truth and the life. No one comes to the Father except through me" (14:6).

"I am the vine; you are the branches. If you remain in me and I in you, you will bear much fruit; apart from me you can do nothing" (15:5).

◆ What does it mean that Jesus said he is *the* way to God rather than *a* way to God? How would you explain the difference between the two?

◆ What are some of the ways you've observed the trend toward inclusivity in popular culture? What is the upside as well as the downside of this trend?

◆ Which of the "I am" statements that Jesus made stands out to you the most? Why are you drawn to that particular statement from Christ?

◆ Clearly, Jesus was using figures of speech in these statements because he is not literally bread, light, a gate, a shepherd, or a vine. Does this change the way you interpret his statement that he is "the way"? Why or why not?

QUESTIONING THE TRUTH

One of the primary objections that people have against Jesus are his claims of exclusivity. Most people like the way he lived. They like the way he loved others. They're just not crazy about him claiming in such definitive terms that he is the only way to salvation.

Perhaps Jesus' statements cause you concern as well. Maybe you struggle to understand how a loving God would provide only one way to heaven. When you hear others say that all paths lead to God, it sounds so compassionate—and you want to be compassionate. And aren't followers of Jesus *supposed* to be compassionate? Shouldn't we take the position that gives hope to the most people? Why would we want to be exclusive? As long as someone believes in doing good and caring about others, isn't that enough, regardless of why they're doing it?

Unfortunately not. What matters is not only the sincerity of our faith but also the trustworthiness of the what—and who—in which we put that faith. While we respect the freedom that people have to choose which religion they will follow, this freedom of choice doesn't mean that all options are equally true. Anyone who claims this hasn't closely studied world religions. While there are some similarities among them, they are dramatically different at their core. If we're all truly worshiping the same God—if we're all just taking different paths to the same God—then that God is either a liar or schizophrenic.

Just consider the tenets of the major religions, starting with the question of in what form God exists. Christianity teaches there is *one* God. Buddhism teaches there is *no* God. Hinduism teaches there are *many* gods—in fact, thousands upon thousands of gods.

There are other major differences as well. Islam states that God told Muhammad every believer must make a pilgrimage to Mecca to worship. Christianity states that Jesus said it doesn't matter where we worship. Hinduism teaches that eating meat is immoral. Christianity teaches it's okay to eat meat. Buddhism claims that when people die, they get reincarnated and live another life on earth. Christianity claims that people live only one life, but that God has invited them to continue living with him forever. New Age belief systems propose that everything in existence is connected to a greater universal whole—and our goal should be to attain a higher consciousness to affect our own transformation. Christianity says there is a personal God who loves us and sent his Son to sacrifice himself for us—and our goal should be to know, love, worship, and glorify this God who brings about his transformation in us.

When put side by side like this, we can easily spot the differences. So, given these comparisons, how can we say that all religions are basically saying the same thing? How could the same God teach all these contradicting ideas? While we might be confused, there is no confusion with God. He is outside of chronological time as we know it and remains the same "yesterday and today and forever" (Hebrews 13:8).

Even if we don't like it, the truth is that there are a lot of people whose faith is in the wrong place. Jesus is who he said he is—the Son of God and the only way to the Father. Christianity's claim that Jesus is the only way is based not on arrogance but on objective evidence, including the evidence of historical events, the teachings of Jesus, the resurrection of Jesus, and the experience of grace through the power of God's Spirit living in us.

◆ Based on your reading in chapter 5 and any online research you want to do, fill in the chart below comparing the core tenets of the world's major religions.

BELIEFS ABOUT GOD	SPIRITUAL PRACTICES	CODE OF CONDUCT	AFTERLIFE
Christianity:			
Buddhism:			
Hinduism:			
Islam:			
New Age:			

◆ Looking over your chart, which differences stand out the most to you? Why?

◆ What are the key distinctions of the Christian faith as compared to the other religions?

◆ With such vast differences, why do you think that so many people still want to believe that all religions lead to God?

DIGGING DEEPER INTO DOUBT

Christianity begs to be investigated. Many intelligent skeptics have looked deeply into whether the events described in the Gospels really happened and ended up putting their faith in Christ. Jesus told people he would die and then, on the third day, rise from the dead (see Matthew 16:21–23; 17:22–23; 20:17–19). And that is what he did! This is the basis for the Christian faith.

Think about that statement. Christianity is not just centered on the *teachings* of Jesus. It's based on his *resurrection*. As Paul wrote, "For what I received I passed on to you as of first importance: that Christ died for our sins according to the Scriptures, that he was buried, [and] that he was raised on the third day according to the Scriptures" (1 Corinthians 15:3–4). Paul said that this truth is the "gospel" by which people are saved (see verse 2).

The truth of the gospel is based on the *resurrection*. As Paul taught, "If Christ has not been raised, our preaching is useless and so is your faith. More than that, we are then found to be false witnesses about God, for we have testified about God that he raised Christ from the dead. . . . And if Christ has not been raised, your faith is futile; you are still in your sins. Then those also who have fallen asleep in Christ are lost. If only for this life we have hope in Christ, we are of all people most to be pitied" (1 Corinthians 15:14–15, 17–19).

Paul explained that we believe not because we have faith in the teachings and philosophy of Jesus but because Jesus *proved* he was who he claimed to be by defeating death. If Jesus hadn't risen from the dead, then everything we believe is moot. But since Jesus did rise from the dead, then he has proven himself trustworthy to us, and we should put our faith in him.

What is truly amazing is that no one can disprove that Jesus rose from the dead. In fact, many brilliant, well-educated people have tried to do this over the centuries, only to conclude that Jesus really did conquer death just as he promised. And because of that evidence, he really is the only way to God.[3]

God provided one way in Jesus. When you stop and think about it, this is actually unfair. For if God had chosen to be fair rather than gracious, then everyone would be getting what they deserve—the consequences of their sin, which is death.

◆ How much time and thought have you invested in studying the evidence supporting the Christian faith? What did you discover in your research—and what would you like to know more about?

◆ How does the fact of Jesus' resurrection support the truth of his teachings? How does the resurrection prove that everything Jesus said is true?

◆ If a nonbeliever asked you about evidence for Jesus' resurrection, what would you share? What evidence influenced your decision to accept Christ?

◆ What lingering frustrations or concerns do you have about Jesus being the only way to God? What is it about this aspect of your faith that still troubles you?

DOUBTFUL AT BEST

Instead of focusing on Jesus' claims to be the only way, perhaps we should just be grateful that he provided any way at all. Jesus died for our sins because it *was* the only way. No other human being could offer the sacrifice that Jesus made on our behalf—permanently and eternally. The only way for us to be saved was by Jesus going to the cross to take our sin and experience death in our place. God loves us so much that he was willing to have his Son do that. Jesus is so passionate about us that he would rather die than live without us. So, he did.

This truth highlights the greatest difference between Christianity and the other world religions—a distinction that some people refer to as "do versus done." People who have carefully studied world religions point out that all of them but one rely on what the individual *does*. You know, how the person lives, treats others, and whether he or she follows the religious rules and protocols. All religions except Christianity are based on the individual doing something to *earn* the favor of God. This might mean going on a pilgrimage, or giving to the poor, or maintaining a certain diet, or performing good deeds, or chanting the right words, or going through a series of reincarnations to continually improve his or her karma. The person strives to reach up to God and earn his favor. It's about what he or she can do for God.

But Christianity stands out as the one religion that focuses on what has already been *done*. It's based not on what the person does but on what Jesus has already done at the cross. The Bible teaches that all people have rebelled against God, but God loves them anyway, so he sent Jesus as a substitute to offer them forgiveness for their sins, a relationship with him, and eternal life in heaven. Christianity is all about God reaching down to people and offering them his unearned favor. It's all about what he has done (see Romans 5:8–11).

Jesus paid the price so we could be forgiven, redeemed, and set free. This is called *grace*. And why did he do this for us? Because of his love: "But God demonstrates his own love for us in this: While we were still sinners, Christ died for us" (Romans 5:8).

◆ How does God's love answer the question, "Why would God only provide one way?" How satisfied are you with this answer?

◆ How would you summarize the distinction between religions that focus on *do* and the one religion (Christianity) that focuses on *done*? Why is this difference so crucial to understanding how Jesus is the only way to God?

◆ What do you think appeals to people about religions focused on what they do? Ultimately, what is the big problem with this spiritual merit system?

◆ What appeals to you about the way Christianity focuses on what Jesus has already done? How does what he has done affect the way you live by faith?

NOTES

1. Annie Kitch and Mia Geoly, "Driving in the Right Direction: State Efforts to Combat Wrong-Way Driving," NCSL, June 26, 2023, https://www.ncsl.org/transportation/driving-in-the-right-direction-state-efforts-to-combat-wrong-way-driving.
2. Kitch and Geoly, "Driving in the Right Direction."
3. If you want to explore this further, check out the resources listed in the notes for chapter 5 in *The Benefit of Doubt*.

WHY BELIEVE IN JESUS WHEN HIS FOLLOWERS ARE SUCH HYPOCRITES?

Jesus has unlimited grace for a sinner in need of forgiveness but no tolerance for hypocrisy.

CRAIG GROESCHEL

Based on what you see in the news, encounter on social media, and hear from other believers, there appears to be an epidemic of hypocrisy infecting those who claim to be Christians. Far too many people can name off a list of these hypocritical Christians who make God look unappealing, if not repulsive. You may have a friend who posts Bible verses on social media, but parties hard all weekend. Or know a father who shames his daughter for dressing immodestly but looks at porn while his family sleeps at night. You may have read about a spiritual leader everyone admired until it came out he wasn't living the life he claimed we all should be living.

The impact of this sinful double life often spawns an even greater epidemic of doubt throughout the entire body of believers. The hurt, anger, and betrayal that such actions generate extend well beyond the individuals who are immediately affected and infect countless others with a sense of deep disappointment. They wonder, *How could they have done such a thing? How could they have lied and deceived so many while continuing to lead? How can they call themselves followers of Jesus when they're nothing but hypocrites?*

Chances are you have firsthand experience with being hurt, let down, or disappointed by a Christian you once admired. As believers, we often expect the best of others who are committed to following Jesus and look to them for guidance, accountability, encouragement, and inspiration. While we know better than to put anyone on a pedestal, when someone we've trusted comes crashing down, we just feel shattered.

The sins of a few cause doubts to spread to the many—and we end up wondering how to answer the question, *Why believe in Jesus when so many of his followers are hypocrites?*

◆ How do you respond to the prevalence of Christians being exposed for their sinful behavior? What makes it worse when you learn of leaders who acted hypocritically?

◆ As you see it, what impact does a scandal involving a prominent Christian have on other believers? What impact does it have on those outside the church?

◆ How would you describe your personal experience with disappointment due to the hypocrisy and/or moral failure of a Christian you once looked up to? Which experience has caused you the most anger, sorrow, and doubt?

◆ How do you typically respond to nonbelievers who ask about Christian scandals in the news? Do you tend to explain the situation as you understand it, apologize on behalf of all believers, or denounce and criticize those exposed? Explain your response.

EXPLORING THE TRUTH

False advertising not only breaks federal laws but also erodes consumer trust. After all, why trust a retailer when its claims about its product have been exposed as untrue? If the false claims were unintentional based on inaccurate data, we might be a bit more understanding. If the deception was intentional, we view the offense as more egregious. Either way, these companies don't come across as trustworthy, and we may be hesitant to buy their products.

Sometimes the failures of other Christians have a similar impact. When we trust pastors, leaders, and mentors, we want to believe their lives align with the convictions of the Christian faith. It's no wonder, then, that we're so devastated when spiritual heroes turn out to be embezzlers, adulterers, liars, thieves, abusers, or swindlers. If they are not the faithful, loving, trustworthy followers of Jesus they appeared to be—then who are they? And what kind of faith do they have . . . or did they actually have any real faith at all?

While it may seem strange to think of Jesus as having a marketing department, his followers are called to be his ambassadors—his hands and feet—here on earth. Just as advertising informs potential consumers about the benefits of a certain product, so Christians are to reveal who Jesus is and what the good news looks like in their lives. Every believer is called to be a shining light that illuminates the darkness of the world with the love of Christ (see Matthew 5:14–16). As Jesus said, "As I have loved you, so you must love one another. By this everyone will know that you are my disciples, if you love one another" (John 13:34–35).

But therein lies the problem. Instead of being characterized by the love of Jesus, many who *say* they are Christians make God seem harsh, judgmental, narrow-minded, indifferent, and untrustworthy. Many people have spiritual doubts not because of *Jesus* but because of his *followers*. Instead of showing God as he really is—full of love, grace, and life-giving truth—these individuals give Christianity a bad rap. Reflecting the love of Jesus means reflecting his grace and goodness in how we speak, live, interact, and behave. As the apostle Paul instructed:

> [2] *Teach the older men to be temperate, worthy of respect, self-controlled, and sound in faith, in love and in endurance.*
>
> [3] *Likewise, teach the older women to be reverent in the way they live, not to be slanderers or addicted to much wine, but to teach what is good.* [4] *Then they can*

urge the younger women to love their husbands and children, [5] to be self-controlled and pure, to be busy at home, to be kind, and to be subject to their husbands, so that no one will malign the word of God.

[6] Similarly, encourage the young men to be self-controlled. [7] In everything set them an example by doing what is good. In your teaching show integrity, seriousness [8] and soundness of speech that cannot be condemned, so that those who oppose you may be ashamed because they have nothing bad to say about us.

TITUS 2:2–8

◆ What are some ways that followers of Jesus "advertise" what the Christian faith is all about? What have others noticed about your speech and behavior that reflect your faith?

◆ What does it mean for everyone to know that you follow Jesus by the way you reflect his love? What does this look like on a daily basis?

◆ What stands out for you in Paul's instructions on how to live as one who reflects the love of Jesus? Which qualities do you have that cause you to consider what others might assume about Jesus based on your behavior?

◆ How do you practice living in the way Paul describes without your faith becoming a merit system based on your attitude and actions? How do you put your Christian beliefs into practice in ways that are feasible for you?

QUESTIONING THE TRUTH

It's devastating but true. Many people who identify themselves as followers of Jesus behave in ways that don't reflect his example and his teachings. Instead of being known for love, as Jesus commanded, they are often known for who they hate and what they are against. Their stance toward others ends up being exclusive, hypercritical, and antagonistic.

Jesus commanded his followers to love their enemies (see Matthew 5:44), but that's not typically what we see on social media. Jesus instructed his followers to be peacemakers (see 5:9), yet many believers shout hateful words at protests and rallies. Jesus taught that only people without sin can cast stones of condemnation (see John 8:1–11), but some Christians today don't hesitate to cast such stones on those they view as sinners.

This phenomenon is nothing new. In fact, Jesus once told a parable that illustrated this mix of faithful followers and hypocritical believers. Often called the parable of the weeds, this comparison reflects the disparate kinds of Christ followers who seem to coexist within the same community, church, and culture.

Jesus began by stating there was a man who sowed good seed in his field. But at night, his enemy came and sowed weeds among his wheat. As the seeds began to sprout, there was obviously a problem, and the man realized what had happened. His servants, offering to help, asked him, "Do you want us to go and pull them up?" The man replied, "No . . . because while you are pulling the weeds, you may uproot the wheat with them. Let both grow together until the harvest. At that time I will tell the harvesters: First collect the weeds and tie them in bundles to be burned; then gather the wheat and bring it into my barn" (Matthew 13:28–30).

Wheat and weeds are still growing in the same fields today. But as God's servants, we don't determine the outcome. We are just supposed to take care of the crop. Only God, the one who owns the field, gets the final say. Meanwhile, God loves us all with an everlasting love. He draws people to himself with his unfailing kindness.

◆ Why do you think so many people who claim to follow Jesus act in ways opposite of what he taught? How aware do you think they are of this discrepancy between what they say they believe and how they actually act?

◆ How do you interpret the parable of the weeds? According to the parable, why does God allow both weeds and wheat to coexist in the same field?

◆ Who does Jesus say planted the weeds? What are the implications of this detail as you consider why some people say they believe in Jesus but don't show it with their actions?

◆ What does the conclusion of the parable mean? Why does the man who owns the field allow both the wheat and weeds to grow until the final harvest?

DIGGING DEEPER INTO DOUBT

If you've been hurt, disappointed, or disillusioned by followers of Jesus who didn't seem to be anything like him, then you're not alone. Jesus didn't like it when people claimed one thing but lived a different way. In fact, Jesus never spoke more harshly about anyone in the Gospels than he did against those he called "hypocrites."

For instance, in Matthew 23, we find seven times when Jesus said "woe to you" to the Pharisees. This group of Jewish religious leaders claimed to live in holiness but were actually self-absorbed and self-glorifying. Here is what Jesus said to them on one of those seven occasions: "Woe to you, teachers of the law and Pharisees, you hypocrites! You are like whitewashed tombs, which look beautiful on the outside but on the inside are full of the bones of the dead and everything unclean. In the same way, on the outside you appear to people as righteous but on the inside you are full of hypocrisy and wickedness" (verses 27–28).

Jesus called these Pharisees *hypocrites*. You will find that same word used seventeen times in the Gospels. Each time, it was Jesus who spoke the word. And each time, he used it to describe people who "do not practice what they preach" (verse 3) . . . people for whom "everything they do is done for people to see" (verse 5).

Prior to Jesus using it, the word *hypocrite* was used exclusively for actors who wore masks onstage. The same actor would play several different parts, so for each character, a different mask was worn. Given this, *hypocrite* came to mean "one who wears a mask." By applying this word to the Pharisees, Jesus was accusing them of pretending to be something they were not. Jesus had a zero-tolerance policy for hypocrites.

After all, Jesus already knew that just like every other human being, these Pharisees were sinners. The problem was their constant attempts to cover it up. They presented a false exterior and manipulated the impressions of others. This deception, to Jesus, was what made them hypocrites. He had unlimited grace for sinners but no tolerance for hypocrisy.

◆ Why did Jesus call out the Pharisees in such harsh terms—particularly in light of how he usually spoke with compassion to the sinners he encountered? What was unique about the sin of the Pharisees and Jewish religious leaders?

◆ When Jesus addressed the Pharisees, why do you think he chose to borrow the word *hypocrite* from its use as a dramatic term in theater? How does its meaning fit the sin of the Pharisees so perfectly?

◆ When have you become aware of playing a role or wearing a mask as you presented your Christian faith to other people? What is the distinction between hypocrisy and simply trying to relate to others for the sake of sharing the gospel?

◆ What do you think Jesus wanted to accomplish by calling out the Pharisees as hypocrites?

DOUBTFUL AT BEST

It's not fair to judge Jesus based on a few of his followers. It's not fair to lump them all together, call them all hypocrites, and just reject the Christian faith altogether. This kind of defensive mindset will keep you from Jesus. And that's not fair to you, because you desperately *need* Jesus. Nothing is worth distancing yourself from him.

Perhaps the best way to deal with hypocritical believers is to do what Paul and Barnabas did in Pisidian Antioch when some of the believers there, after being incited by the Jewish leaders, turned against them. These were "God-fearing women of high standing and the leading men of the city" (Acts 13:50). People respected them and listened to them, so when they turned against Paul and Barnabas, many others jumped on their crowd-mentality bandwagon. In the end, these believers "stirred up persecution against Paul and Barnabas, and expelled them from their region" (verse 50).

So what was Paul and Barnabas's next move? Did they defend themselves, or confront their accusers, or try to divide the church? No, they chose the high road: "They shook the dust off their feet as a warning to them and went to Iconium. And the disciples were filled with joy and with the Holy Spirit" (verses 51–52). They decided, *We're not going to let the sins of some keep us from the goodness of God. He didn't let us down; people did. We're going to shake it off.*

The pain, disappointment, and betrayal you feel that was caused by people who said they followed Jesus is no small thing. It may have set you back, cost you greatly, robbed you of your innocence, and caused you pain. That pain can be excruciating. But at some point, you will realize that God wants you to heal, move on, and get better. In other words, there comes a time when you, too, have to shake off the dust of others' hypocrisy and move on.

If you've been mistreated, betrayed, or abused, it's going to take a lot of praying, and then some shaking, and maybe some counseling, and then more shaking, and then some more praying and introspection, and then more shaking. It won't be easy, but at some point, for your sake, you've got to get where you can shake it off. Find the ability to forgive and let it go and then, like Paul and Barnabas, move on filled with the joy of the Holy Spirit.

HYPOCRISY INVENTORY

If you've ever attended a Twelve Steps recovery meeting or supported someone in a journey of recovery, you know that part of the process (Step 4) requires a "fearless moral inventory" of the ways you have been harmed as well as the harm you have caused others. One of the components of this inventory focuses on resentments, especially toward those who have hurt you over the course of your life. Borrowing from this practice, think about the people, groups, churches, and situations that have caused you grief because of the hypocrisy you've observed and/or experienced. Use the following diagram to complete your personal Hypocrisy Inventory with the goal of releasing these to God, shaking them off, and moving into forgiveness and healing.

People I know personally whose hypocrisy has hurt me:

Pastors, ministry leaders, and prominent Christians whose hypocrisy has hurt me:

Other people whose hypocrisy has hurt me:

Groups/institutions whose hypocrisy has hurt me:

Churches/ministries whose hypocrisy has hurt me:

Situations/events/experiences when hypocrisy has hurt me:

◆ People may disappoint you, but Jesus will never let you down. He is always faithful, trustworthy, unchanging, and loving toward you. How does knowing this about his character help you to forgive those who have wronged you?

WHY DOES GOD FEEL SO FAR AWAY?

If God seems far away, remind yourself that just because he feels distant, it doesn't mean he is absent.

CRAIG GROESCHEL

W hat is the farthest you've ever been stranded away from home? Five hundred miles? One thousand miles? If you've traveled internationally, the distance might be even greater.[1]

Frank Rubio, a military veteran who served as a Black Hawk helicopter pilot and flight surgeon, once found himself stranded about 250 miles from home—though the distance felt indescribably farther. The reason is because those 250 miles spanned the distance between the earth's surface and the International Space Station (ISS).[2]

In 2023, Rubio, an astronaut for NASA, broke the record for the longest trip in space by an American: 371 days aboard the ISS. For more than a year, he made almost six thousand orbits around the earth and traveled more than 157 million miles. His mission was initially slated for six months, but the transport spacecraft began leaking coolant and could not safely make the return journey. So Rubio was forced to wait to catch a ride on a Russian spacecraft.[3]

After landing safely, Rubio acknowledged that if he had known his time away from his wife and four kids would have been so long, he would have declined the mission. As he said, "It's been a mixed emotional roller coaster to a certain degree because personally, it was an incredible challenge, and it was difficult." Rubio noted that he filled his extended time in space by focusing on his mission of studying plant and physical science and that he kept a positive attitude by communicating with his loved ones back home. "Professionally, it was incredibly rewarding. It's a huge honor and it's a privilege to represent our office and our team this way."[4]

When it comes to your faith, you might often feel that you are "stranded" far away from God. Maybe you once felt close to him and regularly experienced his presence, but now you've gone through periods where it feels like he is in a galaxy far, far, far away. You wonder why some moments when you would expect to be close with him—such as a worship service, prayer group, or spiritual retreat—have left you feeling empty.

When God seems so far away, how can you find him? How do you close the distance between where you are and where he is? And *why* does he feel so distant in the first place?

◆ What is the farthest you have gotten stuck away from home? What happened that resulted in you being temporarily stranded there?

◆ How would you have felt if you had been in Frank Rubio's boots? How do you think you would have handled feelings of loneliness, fear, anger, frustration, and disappointment?

◆ When was the last time you felt close to God and sensed his presence? What were the circumstances surrounding that particular experience with him?

◆ When was the last time you felt that God was far away? What feelings did you have as you experienced this sense of distance from him?

EXPLORING THE TRUTH

Think about the last time you got together with a friend you've known for a long time. There is a sense of connection with each other—an ability to just be yourselves and feel known, accepted, enjoyed, and loved. When it's time for your friend to go, you hug and acknowledge the imminent sadness of missing each other until the next visit.

If you can recall connecting with a friend like that, or at least imagine it, then you probably have a good idea how it feels to experience relational closeness. We all have ways we bond with family, close friends, and loved ones. Experiencing closeness with God, however, is more difficult to pin down. Think about this in your life. Do you believe that you have felt the presence of God at some point—a time when you knew he was there with you? How did you know? What made you so sure that you were experiencing connection with God?

Many Christians report experiencing feelings of peace, love, belonging, calmness, awe, and joy when they are in God's presence. Perhaps you've experienced these feelings—and maybe even in a way that transcended the challenging circumstances of your life at that time. How reliable and consistent are those indicators? Does a lack of any of these feelings, or any other emotions for that matter, indicate that God was *not* present with you?

Part of the problem in trying to assess God's closeness stems from our human bodies, minds, and senses. His presence can certainly evoke certain emotions and sensations within us. But so can certain medications along with chemicals the body releases—such the rush of endorphins after a long workout. (This contributes to a feeling of euphoria after a period of exercise that is often known as the "runner's high.") Furthermore, feelings of joy, peace, love, and belonging might indicate we are experiencing God's presence, but it could also be residual effects of watching that Christmas movie with loved ones. The calmness we sense might be God, but it could also stem from a number of other factors in your day.

So, what do you do when you want to *feel* the presence of God—but you don't? If you are asking this question, know that—once again!—you are not alone. A number of people in the Bible felt the same way. David, the "man after [God's] own heart" (Acts 13:22), likely spoke more about feeling God's presence than anyone else in the Bible. In particular, the psalms he wrote reflect the extremes he felt when it came to experiencing God. At one end of these extremes, you will find passages such as this one:

> *7 I will bless the LORD who guides me;*
> *even at night my heart instructs me.*
> *8 I know the LORD is always with me.*
> *I will not be shaken, for he is right beside me.*
> *9 No wonder my heart is glad, and I rejoice.*
> *My body rests in safety.*
>
> PSALM 16:7–9 NLT

And at the other end, you will find passages that express just the opposite:

> *8 I am in a trap with no way of escape.*
> *9 My eyes are blinded by my tears.*
> *Each day I beg for your help, O LORD;*
> *I lift my hands to you for mercy. . . .*
> *13 O LORD, I cry out to you.*
> *I will keep on pleading day by day.*
> *14 O LORD, why do you reject me?*
> *Why do you turn your face from me?*
>
> PSALM 88:8–9, 13–14 NLT

◆ How would you describe the ways you've experienced God's presence in your life? What common elements do you see among your various experiences?

◆ When have you longed to *connect* with God—to feel his peace and comfort and know his unconditional love—and yet there was nothing? How have you typically responded in those moments of longing for more from God?

◆ When you are struggling to feel close to God, do you tend to assume the problem is with you? Or do you wonder what's going on with God? Explain your answer.

◆ Which of the two passages from the book of Psalms resonates the most with you right now? Knowing that David was just as human as you are, how was he able to feel such intimacy with God at certain times and then wonder if God was even there at other times?

QUESTIONING THE TRUTH

David certainly understood what it was like to feel far away from God—and he even cried out to the Lord to make himself known. But there is a more surprising person in the Bible who also knew what it was like to feel separation from God the Father. This person was none other than Jesus. During Jesus' time on earth, he said, "The Father and I are one" (John 10:30 NLT). The Father and Son walked intimately with each other every day of Jesus' life. Christ's mission was to glorify his Father in every way, and he was obedient even to death.

We see this in the fact that Jesus was willing to be insulted, mocked, and crucified as a sacrifice for our sin. As Paul wrote, it was there on the cross that "God made him who had no sin to be sin for us, so that in him we might become the righteousness of God" (2 Corinthians 5:21). The Father did not abandon his Son in that moment, but neither could his holiness be in the presence of the sin that Jesus willingly took upon himself.[5] So, in some way that we cannot possibly understand, God removed his presence from his Son as he hung on the cross.

It must have been unbearable for Jesus. We know this, in part, because he cried out, "My God, my God, why have you forsaken me?" (Matthew 27:46). *Jesus knew what it felt like to not feel the presence of God.* For this reason, we can be certain that he understands what it is like for us when we also do not feel the presence of God. As we read in Hebrews, "We do not have a high priest who is unable to empathize with our weaknesses" (4:15).

Sometimes, our imaginations inflate our expectations of what it is like to experience God's presence. We want God to announce that he is near to us with signs like manna from heaven, water from a rock, or fireproof strolls through burning coals. Although these signs and wonders have happened, they are not typically going to be the way that most of us will encounter God's presence. And this might actually be a good thing.

Why? Because Jesus warned us to be careful about requiring signs from God. On one occasion, the Pharisees and Sadducees asked Jesus to show them a sign that proved God was present with him. Jesus responded, "A wicked and adulterous generation looks for a sign, but none will be given it except the sign of Jonah" (Matthew 16:4). The "sign of Jonah" was that Jesus would walk out of his grave—not the belly of a whale—three days after being buried. He was telling them that his resurrection was all they really needed as proof.

Our feelings are not the only evidence of God's presence. If we always felt God, we wouldn't need faith. So, when we are not feeling closeness with God, we need to ask if we are expecting something *sensational* instead of something *relational*.

◆ Why was it necessary for God to remove his presence from Jesus as he hung on the cross? How does Jesus' willingness to suffer this feeling of forsakenness help you relate to him?

◆ Why is biblical proof of God's presence more significant than your feelings of God's presence? When is a time that your feelings led you astray in this regard?

◆ Why did Jesus warn the Pharisees and Sadducees to not look for signs as confirmation of God's presence? What does the "sign of Jonah"—Jesus' sacrifice on the cross and victory over death so we could be reconciled with God—reveal about your heavenly Father's desire to be close to you?

◆ What part does faith play in acknowledging that God is always near? What are some passages from the Bible that have reassured you that God is always close to you?

DIGGING DEEPER INTO DOUBT

When you are struggling to experience God's presence, remember what is true about your relationship with him: "Yet now he has reconciled you to himself through the death of Christ in his physical body. As a result, he has brought you into his own presence, and you are holy and blameless as you stand before him without a single fault" (Colossians 1:22 NLT).

God has brought us into his presence. Furthermore, we have the assurance that we can "approach God's throne of grace with confidence, so that we may receive mercy and find grace to help us in our time of need" (Hebrews 4:16). God is always available to us and with us—whether we feel it or not. Sometimes, as we've said, it takes faith and trusting that he is there.

However, as we learn to rely on our faith, we need to acknowledge that sometimes the Holy Spirit will reveal that there is a problem in our relationship with the Lord. Jesus said, "The Advocate, the Holy Spirit, whom the Father will send in my name, will teach you all things and will remind you of everything I have said to you" (John 14:26). Sometimes, the Holy Spirit will reveal that we have become hard-hearted toward God and need "a new heart" (Ezekiel 36:26).

Jesus described the result of a hardened heart when he said, "You will be ever hearing but never understanding; you will be ever seeing but never perceiving. For this people's heart has become calloused; they hardly hear with their ears, and they have closed their eyes" (Matthew 13:14–15). How does a heart become hardened toward God like this? While there are many factors, some of the biggest ones include bitterness, resentment, and accepting sinfulness—particularly sinfulness stemming from anger, lust, jealousy, and greed. We live in a culture that reinforces our natural tendencies toward sin and has even made it into entertainment. It's everywhere and accepted—and sometimes celebrated.

Don't buy into the lie that sin is okay. You can't justify it, make excuses for it, or accept it as a part of who you are if you want to experience closeness with God. You must watch out for the warning signs that you are rationalizing sin—statements you make to yourself such as, *Oh, that's just how I roll*, or, *What's it going to hurt—people are guilty of this every day*, or, *This isn't so bad when you consider what everybody else is doing.*

Such justification of sin will calcify your ability to know God because it will allow a layer of sin to create some distance. God hasn't moved away—*you* will have drifted away because of the pull of accepting sin. So, what is the remedy for a hardened heart? Simply to repent and accept God's forgiveness. Regardless of how you feel, repentance is a choice to return to him after straying in your own direction. He is still with you—and he wants you to be with him.

◆ How important are feelings to you in knowing that you are secure in your relationship with God? Why is it important not to rely on feelings if you want your faith to grow?

◆ When have you sensed that your heart might be hardening toward God? What causes played a part in allowing this to happen?

◆ Which struggles in your life have the greatest potential to harden your heart toward God? How do you remain spiritually attentive to resist temptation and avoid a hardened heart?

◆ When was the last time you identified complacency regarding sinfulness in your life? What measures did you take to restore your relationship with God?

DOUBTFUL AT BEST

God wants us to stay close to him and be dependent on him. The problem is that we often keep our distance from him and live independently of him—that is, until we realize we need him. Because of this tendency, God will lead us to seek him.

God does not need anything from us, but we always need him. One time, when Paul was finding common ground with his listeners in Athens, he said, "[God] himself gives everyone life and breath and everything else. . . . God did this so that [people] would seek him and perhaps reach out for him and find him, though he is not far from any one of us" (Acts 17:25, 27).

Notice what Paul said: *God is not far from any one of us*. God wants you to seek him, reach out to him, and find him. So, perhaps he has let you get to a point where you long to be closer with him. Those feelings of estrangement from him are intended to cause you to seek him. It's when you're feeling desperate that you're most likely to recognize your need for him.

Consider it this way. If you're deprived of something you need, you usually recognize the impact of your deficiency and do something about it. For example, if you don't eat, you get hungry and are motivated to eat food. If you don't drink, you get thirsty and are motivated to drink. Similarly, when you don't feel God's presence, you're awakened to how bankrupt you are without him. You understand that you need him every moment. You hunger and thirst for him, and so you seek him. And, when you do, you find God, just as he promised: "You will seek me and find me when you seek me with all your heart" (Jeremiah 29:13).

There will be times when God will move in your life in incredible ways. But more often, he desires for you to follow David's prescription: "Be still, and know that I am God" (Psalm 46:10). God loves you and is with you. He has promised to never leave you nor forsake you (see Hebrews 13:5). You can rest in the truth of his promise, no matter how you feel.

◆ What spiritual practices help you sustain a close connection with God? What role do your feelings play in the effectiveness of these practices?

◆ As you consider the content of this lesson, as well as chapter 7 in *The Benefit of Doubt*, what is the biggest takeaway when it comes to experiencing God's ongoing presence?

◆ What are some of the everyday moments lately when you've been aware of God's presence? What prompted your awareness in these moments?

◆ What does it mean for you to be still and know that God is who he says he is? How would you describe your experience of doing this?

NOTES

1. The farthest distance between two cities on earth is from Xinghua, China, to Rosario, Argentina, which are 12,425 miles apart from each other.
2. "How Far Away Is Space?", NASA, https://www.jpl.nasa.gov/edu/resources/lesson-plan/how-far-away-is-space/.
3. Ayana Archie, "A NASA Astronaut Is Back on Earth After a Year in Space, the Longest for an American," NPR, September 28, 2023, https://www.npr.org/2023/09/20/1200374445/nasa-frank-rubio-record-yearlong-flight.
4. Archie, "A NASA Astronaut Is Back on Earth After a Year in Space, the Longest for an American."
5. Billy Graham, "Did God Abandon Jesus on the Cross?" Billy Graham Evangelistic Association, March 24, 2016, https://billygraham.org/story/did-god-abandon-jesus-on-the-cross-billy-graham-answers/.

WHY WOULD GOD SEND PEOPLE TO HELL?

Jesus knew hell was real and wanted the threat to be understood for us to avoid it at any cost.

CRAIG GROESCHEL

The use of profanity on television has certainly come a long way. Most viewers today won't even notice if a character uses the word *hell* as a profane figure of speech. However, viewers back in 1967 did when the original *Star Trek* series concluded with Captain Kirk using the word. Originally broadcast at the end of the first season, "The City on the Edge of Forever" episode introduced all kinds of plot points (including time travel) but was also one of the first—if not *the* first—prime-time television shows with such an utterance by a main character.[1]

Today, when considered as a place—particularly in popular culture and media—hell is often depicted as either incredibly humorous or horrific. In either case, hell usually takes the form of earthly locales and includes what most people would find painful, torturous, and unbearable. Perhaps the most benign depictions show a cartoon hell with horn-and-pitchfork devils joking about the people being punished there. The more disturbing portrayals are found in grisly novels, films, and TV shows rooted in the horror genre.

It is likely that all these different depictions of hell have contributed to people's general confusion about it. They wonder if hell is a literal place or just a state of being. They ponder if hell features unbearable torment for all eternity or if it is just a kind of imprisonment until the inhabitants change their wicked ways. Both Christians and nonbelievers often wonder what to do with references to hell found in the Bible. They struggle to reconcile the mercy of God with the fire of hell. The question that gets asked again and again is: *If God loves us so much that he sent Jesus to pay for our sins, then why would he send anyone to such a horrible place?*

This question of not only *why* God might send someone to hell but also *who* might go there can be so agonizing that it's compelling to want to dismiss the topic altogether. But hell is too big a gamble to ignore! We need to know what will happen to us and the people we love after we die. And while we might want to ignore the prospect of hell, Jesus sure didn't. He talked about hell quite a bit and wanted us to understand it. As uncomfortable as it might make us feel, understanding hell is also about understanding heaven. And, considered together, heaven and hell provide a greater understanding of who God is.

◆ What are some of the depictions of hell that you have seen on television and in movies? How is hell most often depicted in the media?

◆ What specifically has influenced *your* concept of hell as a place? What concerns and questions about hell trouble you the most?

◆ How can understanding the truth about hell strengthen your faith? How can it help motivate you in how you interact with nonbelievers?

◆ On a scale of 1 to 10, with 1 being "doubtful" and 10 being "certain," what score reflects your level of confidence that hell is a real place? Explain your response.

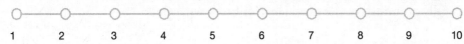

1   2   3   4   5   6   7   8   9   10

EXPLORING THE TRUTH

We can all agree that heaven is a more comfortable topic to consider than hell. This is true even though heaven has likely just as many misconceptions. For instance, many people assume heaven will either be like a never-ending party or the ultimate luxury vacation with all the perks. Who wouldn't want that? Virtually everyone would want to go to that version of heaven!

However, this notion of heaven is mostly rooted in the human imagination. People believe heaven will be like that because they *want* heaven to be like that.

Yet just as we can't make up details about where we live simply because we want to do so, we can't describe heaven in any way we choose.

So, what is heaven? Well, the Bible states that it is a real place where followers of Christ will experience everlasting life with God (see John 3:16). God created human beings to be with him, know him intimately, and experience life with him eternally. But as human beings with free will, we sin, and our sin interferes with our ability to enjoy life with God. So God remedied this problem by sending Jesus to earth to die for our sins so that we might have life with him. This new life with God starts here in the present and continues into eternity.

The Bible teaches that death is not the end for us. It is a doorway to a new and forever kind of life. As John declared, "Look! God's dwelling place is now among the people, and he will dwell with them. They will be his people, and God himself will be with them and be their God" (Revelation 21:3). Recognize the implication here: *Heaven is God dwelling among his people.* Heaven is not about enjoying someplace with all your favorite things. Heaven is about experiencing the joy of life with God. While the Bible references earthly items, the picture of heaven it reveals is fully grounded in the experience of being with God:

> [22] *I did not see a temple in the city, because the Lord God Almighty and the Lamb are its temple.* [23] *The city does not need the sun or the moon to shine on it, for the glory of God gives it light, and the Lamb is its lamp.* [24] *The nations will walk by its light, and the kings of the earth will bring their splendor into it.* [25] *On no day will its gates ever be shut, for there will be no night there.* [26] *The glory and honor of the nations will be brought into it.* [27] *Nothing impure will ever enter it, nor will anyone who does what is shameful or deceitful, but only those whose names are written in the Lamb's book of life.*
>
> REVELATION 21:22–27

Notice that heaven does not contain God—God contains heaven. In heaven, God is everywhere. No matter where you go or what you do, you will not be able to avoid God in heaven. This means that if you're *not* the kind of person who wants to be with God, then you won't enjoy heaven. Or if you're the kind of person who wants to keep *sinning*, then you will be very uncomfortable in heaven. Similarly, if you find yourself sinning in this life but desperately don't want to do so, heaven is going to solve that problem.

Heaven is eternal and uninterrupted life with God. Those who want to be with God will absolutely love it. But those who would rather avoid God will not want to go there.

◆ What comes to mind when you imagine what heaven will be like? What has influenced your understanding of what heaven will be like?

◆ Why is it essential to understand heaven in order to understand hell? How does understanding that heaven is eternal life with God change the way you view it?

◆ What does understanding both heaven and hell reveal about who God is? What does it reveal about who you are and what you ultimately want?

◆ Why would anyone *not* want to go to heaven? Why might someone actually decide that he or she doesn't want to be in heaven with God all the time?

QUESTIONING THE TRUTH

Given this understanding that heaven is eternal life with God, it makes sense that hell represents eternal separation from God's presence. Just as the Bible indicates that heaven is an actual place, so also the Scriptures say that hell is real. While cartoonish images of dungeons ruled by red devils may come to mind, this isn't how the Bible describes hell.

In fact, we might consider whether the enemy has tried to promote the idea that we don't have to take hell seriously. This strategy plays into our discomfort and doubts related to hell. Perhaps Satan wants people to believe that hell is a never-ending party where you can do anything you please with no consequences. You know, that notion of wanting to be in hell with all the fun people instead of in heaven with the uptight Christians.

Such beliefs make it easier for people to reject Jesus and live a sin-justifying, self-centered, comfort-craving, sacrifice-rejecting, persecution-avoiding life—a life spent loving a world that will not last.

Sadly, this is what most people do. Jesus warned us about this when he said, "You can enter God's Kingdom only through the narrow gate. The highway to hell is broad, and its gate is wide for the many who choose that way. But the gateway to life is very narrow and the road is difficult, and only a few ever find it" (Matthew 7:13-14 NLT). In order to choose the gateway to life, we must be mindful of the reality of hell.

As noted previously, the subject of hell comes up quite a bit in the Bible, and Jesus actually talked about it more than anyone. This often surprises people, because Jesus was the most compassionate person who ever lived. But that's exactly why he spoke of hell so often! Because of his love and compassion, he doesn't want anyone to go there.

Jesus knew that hell was real. He wanted the threat of it to be understood so that people would avoid it at any cost. To emphasize this point, he once said, "If your right eye causes you to stumble, gouge it out and throw it away. It is better for you to lose one part of your body than for your whole body to be thrown into hell" (Matthew 5:29). The word Jesus used for *hell* is the Greek word *Gehenna*, which was an actual place in Jerusalem.

This area in the southwest corner of the city was known as the Valley of Hinnom. Centuries before Jesus, King Ahaz worshiped the god Molech there with child sacrifices (see Jeremiah 7:31). Due to its evil history, Gehenna became a garbage dump where people tossed dead animals, human waste, sewage, and the bodies of executed criminals. The waste was burned with a smoldering fire—and the whole area carried a terrible stench.

This is the place Jesus used as a reference point for hell. Gehenna depicts a desolate place without beauty, laughter, friendship, peace, joy, or hope of escape or rescue. Jesus made it clear that hell is a place cut off from God's presence and everything good. Just as heaven is life *with* God, so hell is life *without* God.

◆ Why do you think Jesus instructed us to consider extreme measures—such as gouging out our eye if it causes us to sin—rather than risk suffering in hell?

◆ When you consider Gehenna as the place Jesus referenced as hell, what comes to mind? What place have you seen that reminds you of Gehenna?

◆ Why is it impossible for all that is good, beautiful, loving, and joyful to exist in hell? Why is it impossible for evil, sin, shame, and sorrow to be found in heaven?

◆ How do you respond to the fact that Jesus talked about hell more than anyone else in the Bible? In what ways was his willingness to talk about hell motivated by his compassion for people?

DIGGING DEEPER INTO DOUBT

We are eternal creatures, so after this life we need someplace to live out our eternities. God's hope is that everyone will choose to be with him in heaven. But for those who reject him, he honors their free will to choose hell as the place where they can reside eternally.

Hell also exists as the place where God will punish Satan (see Revelation 20:10). Rather than a cartoon devil, Satan embodies every addiction and abuse. He is behind all fear and shame and pain. In the Bible he is called a serpent, a tempter, a thief, a roaring lion, an accuser, and the father of lies.[2] His mission is to steal, kill, and destroy (see John 10:10).

Those who reject God are basically choosing to be with Satan. In one story, Jesus told about what happened to two different individuals after they died. The first was "a rich man who was dressed in purple and fine linen and lived in luxury every day" (Luke 16:19). The second was a poor man named Lazarus who sat at the gate of this rich guy's property. He was so hungry he longed for the crumbs the stray dogs ate—the same dogs that licked his sores.

When Lazarus died, the angels carried him to "Abraham's side" in heaven (verse 22). When the rich man died, he was taken to Hades, which was known as the place of punishment for the dead. There in Hades, where the rich man was "in torment" (verse 23), he looked up and saw Abraham next to Lazarus. So he called out, "Father Abraham, have pity on me and send Lazarus to dip the tip of his finger in water and cool my tongue, because I am in agony in this fire" (verse 24). The rich man wanted a little relief from his suffering.

Abraham told him this was not possible: "Son, remember that in your lifetime you received your good things, while Lazarus received bad things, but now he is comforted here and you are in agony" (verse 25). So the rich man then made a different request: "I beg you, father, send Lazarus to my family, for I have five brothers. Let him warn them, so that they will not also come to this place of torment" (verses 27–28).

Notice that the rich man was fully aware of why he was experiencing what he was experiencing. He recognized the punishment was fair, despite how excruciating it was to endure. He evidently now regretted how he had lived on earth, but it was too late to change. So he pleaded for someone to help his brothers escape the same consequences that he was facing.

As self-consumed as he may have been, the rich guy still loved his brothers. When you love someone, you desperately don't want them to go to hell—which is why we must be willing to talk about it.

◆ Why is hell the only place adequate for punishing Satan? How does hell serve as a suitable place for all the evil, harm, and destruction the enemy has caused?

◆ Why is it important for people to realize that rejecting God means choosing to be with Satan in hell? What difference does this make in how you understand the necessity of hell?

◆ What grabs your attention in the story that Jesus told about the rich man and the beggar named Lazarus? What does this story reveal about hell?

◆ How does the rich man's request for his brothers to be warned about hell motivate you to help others escape its torment as well?

DOUBTFUL AT BEST

God gave you free will to choose life with him or without him. God sent his Son, Jesus, so you would know how much he loves you. He has provided a way—no matter what you've done—to be with him in eternity. Hell exists because there has to be a place for God to righteously punish evil—and our sin is evil.

The Bible is clear that "all have sinned and fall short of the glory of God" (Romans 3:23). *All* includes everyone—even you. No matter how many good deeds you've done or how hard you've tried to be a good person, it's not enough. Jesus is the only way for you to escape the just punishment for your sins.

While this is not pleasant to think about, we all must come to terms with our sin. God originally made us "very good" (Genesis 1:31), and "we are God's masterpiece" (Ephesians 2:10 NLT). But then we went astray. On our own, we're not capable of doing the good we were made for. All our best motivations are shot through with sin. Only God is 100 percent good, through and through.

On our own, we are not holy. We are called to holiness (see 1 Peter 1:16), but we are not able to come anywhere near it without God's work in us. Only God is 100 percent holy with no help from anyone else. And he makes us holy when we surrender our lives and hearts to him.

Because God is good and holy, he must also be just. And because he is just, he must punish sin. But God is also love, and because he loves us, he sent Jesus: "But God demonstrates his own love for us in this: While we were still sinners, Christ died for us" (Romans 5:8). Jesus' death and resurrection make all the difference.

Even though we all sin, God wants us to know, "All are justified freely by his grace through the redemption that came by Christ Jesus. God presented Christ as a sacrifice of atonement, through the shedding of his blood—to be received by faith" (Romans 3:24–25). No matter how gross our sin, God's grace is greater and covers all our sins.

Furthermore, when we confess our sins and hand everything over to God, he is faithful and just to forgive us (see 1 John 1:9). Jesus offers grace, not guilt or grief. There is now no condemnation for those who, through their faith, are in Christ (see Romans 8:1).

So, the answer to the question as to why God would send someone to hell is that he doesn't. People choose hell. They choose hell when they reject life with God and decide to live as their own god. They choose hell whenever they deny their sin. They choose hell when they say no to Jesus and what he did on the cross for them.

Hell is the place where people must pay for their sins if they choose not to allow Jesus to pay for them. Again, God doesn't want *anyone* to go to hell, which is why he sent Jesus for everyone. As Peter wrote, "The Lord is not slow in keeping his promise, as some understand slowness. Instead he is patient with you, not wanting anyone to perish, but everyone to come to repentance" (2 Peter 3:9). God wants *everyone* to come to repentance.

God is patient with you. He's waiting for you. He's working in you. He's reaching out to you. He's sending people your way. He has sent this book your way! He's drawing you to himself by his Spirit. The same is true for those you love who don't know Jesus. He's patient with them, waiting for them, and drawing them by his Spirit. He wants them free from the pain of sin so they can experience his goodness on earth and for eternity.

The devil comes to steal, kill, and destroy. Jesus came that people might have abundant life. No one has to choose hell, because Jesus came to give us eternal life with God.

◆ How would you explain to a nonbeliever that God doesn't send people to hell but that it is the consequence of rejecting a relationship with him through Christ? What questions or rebuttals would you anticipate that person having?

◆ How does the existence of hell actually reveal the extent to which God loves you? How did Jesus overcome the claim hell has on people once and for all?

◆ What do you want others, particularly nonbelievers you know, to understand about hell? Why is it important that they have an accurate grasp on hell?

NOTES

1. Edward Gross and Mark A. Altman, *Captains' Logs: The Unauthorized Complete Trek Voyages* (New York: Little Brown & Company, 1995), 42.
2. *Serpent*: Genesis 3:1 and Revelation 12:9; *tempter*: Matthew 4:3; *thief*: John 10:10; *roaring lion*: 1 Peter 5:8; *accuser*: Revelation 12:10; *father of lies*: John 8:44.

WHY BELIEVE THE BIBLE IF SCIENCE CONTRADICTS IT?

The God of science is also the God of the Bible. He's given us both, and each is meant to reveal him to us.

CRAIG GROESCHEL

I n the spring of 1925, the Tennessee state legislature passed a bill, known as the Butler Act, that made it illegal for public school educators to teach any doctrine in conflict with the divine creation of human beings as revealed in the Bible. The law resulted from the growing public awareness of Charles Darwin's theory of evolution. While Darwin's seminal work *On the Origin of Species* had first been published in 1859, its impact only grew slowly as scientists, biologists, and anthropologists begin to increasingly support its basic premise of evolution.[1]

The Butler Act soon became the lightning rod for a legal showdown between two camps: one supporting the freedom of educators to teach science without restraint from the church or government, and the other supporting the need to maintain the Bible as the final authority for truth. This showdown occurred when a high school teacher named John T. Scopes was charged with violating the law by teaching Darwin's theory.[2]

Nicknamed the "Scopes Monkey Trial," the case had legal, educational, and cultural repercussions that continue to this day. The trial showcased the scientific evidence for evolution as well as the significance of how the Bible should be interpreted.[3] It continues to provide insight into the ongoing clash between science and the Bible.

You likely have encountered this clash in some form in your own life. The tension reflects the tug-of-war that often takes place between knowledge and faith. As an educated person, you're interested in scientific evidence and where it leads. And as a follower of Jesus, you love the life-giving truth of Scripture.

When the two seem to contradict, you probably feel as if something has to give. You might question both and wonder if you can trust the reliability of either one. But what if science and the Bible are more *complementary* than contradictory? What if they are not competitive but *cooperative* in revealing what is true? What if science and the Bible can actually work *together* to help you grow closer to God and get stronger in your faith?

◆ What were the issues at stake in the famous Scopes Monkey Trial? Which of these issues do you feel remain relevant even today?

◆ How have you handled situations where you've encountered a conflict between what science teaches and what the Bible teaches? What impact have such conflicts had on your faith?

◆ When was the last time you noticed tension between scientific knowledge and the truth of God's Word? What were the circumstances—and who else was involved?

◆ How important is it for you to reconcile science and the Bible in order to grow in your faith? How much of a barrier has it been for trusting God?

EXPLORING THE TRUTH

Here is an important point we need to make up front: *The God of science is also the God of the Bible.* He has given us both, and both are meant to reveal him to us. We fall into a trap when we assume our choice of one precludes the other. God is the author and creator of *both* the Bible and all of creation. He has revealed himself through nature and through the Bible. You might say that has given us two books: the "book" of God's world and the book of God's Word—written by the same sovereign author—that go together hand in hand.

Paul realized this connection when he wrote, "For ever since the world was created, people have seen the earth and sky. Through everything God made, they can clearly see his invisible qualities—his eternal power and divine nature. So they have no excuse for not knowing God" (Romans 1:20 NLT). We also find this truth—that God reveals himself through his creation—reflected in many of the psalms, including this one written by David:

> [1] *The heavens proclaim the glory of God.*
>   *The skies display his craftsmanship.*
> [2] *Day after day they continue to speak;*
>   *night after night they make him known.*
> [3] *They speak without a sound or word;*
>   *their voice is never heard.*
> [4] *Yet their message has gone throughout the earth,*
>   *and their words to all the world. . . .*
>
> [7] *The instructions of the LORD are perfect,*
>   *reviving the soul.*
> *The decrees of the LORD are trustworthy,*
>   *making wise the simple.*
> [8] *The commandments of the LORD are right,*
>   *bringing joy to the heart.*
> *The commands of the LORD are clear,*
>   *giving insight for living. . . .*
> [9] *The laws of the LORD are true;*
>   *each one is fair.*
> [10] *They are more desirable than gold,*
>   *even the finest gold.*
> *They are sweeter than honey,*
>   *even honey dripping from the comb.*

PSALM 19:1–4, 7–10 NLT

So, God is the God of science *and* the God of Scripture. A belief that they are in conflict comes from misunderstanding one or the other. The truth is not found in science or the Bible. The truth is found in science *and* the Bible.

◆ How do you respond to this idea that science and the Bible *both* reveal God's truth? What has made it challenging for you to believe this?

◆ How have you experienced the way God's creation reveals his character? What divine qualities of God do you see displayed in the natural world around you?

◆ How does Psalm 19 connect the truth of God found in his creation with the truth of God found in his Word? Why did David emphasize both of them in the same psalm?

◆ What questions come to mind as you consider that God reveals truth in both science and the Bible? What has influenced you to believe that the two cannot both be true?

QUESTIONING THE TRUTH

One reason that some people believe the Bible and science are at odds, or that science has disproven the Bible, is because they don't have clarity on what each is really about. In one sense, both God's Word and science are similar in that, at their core, they both present truth. However, this can lead to confusion when each, in presenting truth, seems to offer different answers. How is this possible? Because they're not centered on the same kind of truth.

Science is based on what *can* be observed. The scientific method begins with an observation, which then raises a question, which leads to a hypothesis. To test the hypothesis, an experiment is conducted, and its data analyzed to see if it supports or refutes the hypothesis. Science is defined by—and limited to—that which can be observed.

Faith is based on what *cannot* be observed. The truth of the Bible has to be taken by faith. As we're told, "faith is confidence in what we hope for and assurance about what we do not see" (Hebrews 11:1). Later in that same chapter, we read that Moses, one of the fathers of our faith, "persevered because he saw him who is invisible" (verse 27). In describing Christians, the Bible reinforces this truth: "For we live by faith, not by sight" (2 Corinthians 5:7).

Faith is about believing in and living for something that is not observable, measurable, or repeatable. As Paul wrote, "When you received [God's] message from us, you didn't think of our words as mere human ideas. You accepted what we said as the very word of God—which, of course, it is. And this word continues to work in you who believe" (1 Thessalonians 2:13 NLT).

So, science and Scripture employ different *methods* in helping people discover what is the truth. For this reason, they will not always come to the same conclusions. However, this doesn't mean that the two are at odds, nor does it mean the different answers they find are mutually exclusive. For instance, science is an effective tool in revealing truths about the natural world, but that does not mean the supernatural world the Bible teaches does not exist. Scripture is our source for spiritual truth, but relying on its authority does not negate what science reveals.

Science seeks truth about our natural world. Scripture is a different tool that reveals truth about the supernatural world. Science and Scripture can and do work together. Why? Because they point us to the same God. We can therefore conclude by saying the goal of science is to produce *clarity*, while the goal of the Bible is to produce *faith*.

◆ How would you explain the different approaches that science and the Bible take to reveal what is true? Why are the two approaches not mutually exclusive?

◆ How much do you trust science as a reliable source of truth? How much do you trust Scripture as a reliable source of truth? On a scale of 1 to 10, with 1 being "very little" and 10 being "completely," what scores reflect your answers?

| 1 | 2 | 3 | 4 | 5 | 6 | 7 | 8 | 9 | 10 |

◆ While it is evident how the Bible points us to God, what are some ways that science also points us to him? What is one scientific area that reveals an aspect of God to you?

◆ In what ways does science provide *clarity* on our natural world? In what ways does the Bible produce *faith* in a person? How do these two work together?

DIGGING DEEPER INTO DOUBT

Perhaps you've been looking for clarity your whole life. You want to have an unquestionably clear grasp on what life is on this earth. That's not bad. It's good. Keep looking! But at some point, you are going to realize that what you need more than clarity is faith.

Also, you are going to realize at some point that Christianity is not about having all the right answers. Rather, Christianity is about having faith in Jesus, which will give you a vital relationship with God. He is the one who *does* hold all the answers.

Clarity and "right" answers follow the scientific approach, not the faith-filled one. If you feel you have to have every right answer when it comes to your faith, you may be building it on your own understanding instead of on the person of Christ. When this happens and one of your beliefs about God is challenged, it can cause your entire faith system to crumble.

Remember, with the scientific method, you start with a hypothesis and then run an experiment to test it. This produces a result that leads you to a conclusion. If your hypothesis is disproven, do you give up on science? No! You come up with a different hypothesis, which then leads to more questions as you pursue a deeper understanding. You then come up with a new hypothesis and do another test to determine whether you got it right this time.

Why not take the same approach when it comes to your faith? If you recognize there is a challenge to one of your beliefs about God, don't just give up on God. View it as an opportunity to grow. Ask more questions and consider other ways of addressing those challenges. Pursue a deeper understanding of what the Bible says and who God really is. Don't just walk away from God because something wasn't exactly the way you thought.

God and his Word are *infallible*. However, your human understanding of God's Word is *fallible*. You have limitations, and the way you process ideas will get colored by your education, experiences, and relationships. So, in order to keep trusting God, you basically need to keep applying the scientific method to your faith.

If you're not convinced, just consider some of the ways that humankind's understanding of the natural world has changed over time. For instance, Thales of Miletus (625–547 BC), who was widely known in antiquity for his ideas about the earth, believed our planet floated on a massive body of water.[4] The astronomer

Ptolemy (AD 100–170) believed the earth was the center of the universe.[5] The physicist Robert Boyle (1627–1691) was a proponent of the luminiferous aether theory, which held that the earth moved through a "medium" of aether that carried light.[6] All of these beliefs were eventually challenged and disproven.

You are never going to have perfect clarity or get all the answers exactly right. This is why you must believe by *faith*. You can rely on the Bible as your source for trusting in what you cannot always observe, test, analyze, and assess.

◆ What experience, event, or conversation once challenged your beliefs about God and the Bible? How has your view of this challenge changed over time?

◆ How would you describe the "scientific method" as it relates to the natural world? What happens in the scientific community when a particular hypothesis is challenged?

◆ How have you used the scientific method (even if you didn't call it that) to grow in your faith? What do you do when a "hypothesis," or belief you held, is challenged?

◆ What beliefs within your faith have changed the most since you first began following Jesus? Why have they changed?

DOUBTFUL AT BEST

More and more scientists today are affirming what the Bible has held to be true for a long time. For one, researchers have established what is known as the "anthropic principle"—which is that the universe appears to be designed for human life. Cumulative research in astronomy and physics has revealed the emergence of human civilization required certain constants, laws, and properties—and that the earth is narrowly suited for such development to occur.

From the tilt of its axis, to the speed at which it rotates, to its distance from the sun, the earth seems designed for human existence. And it should—because the Bible says God created both the earth and the people inhabiting it. The chances of such a near-perfect design happening randomly amounts to a near impossibility. We, of course, know there was nothing random about it. God created the heavens and earth and said it was good. Natural creation, in all its intricacy, delicacy, practicality, and brilliance, reflects the divinity of its Creator. "The heavens declare the glory of God; the skies proclaim the work of his hands" (Psalm 19:1).

Science, as more and more evidence is collected, will help you understand the truth of this statement. Rather than cause you to question your faith, it can actually increase your confidence in your faith. Yet science has its limits! It can give you some answers about the natural world, but it can never give you a forever relationship with a supernatural God. Something you see in the field of science might be a catalyst for pointing you to God—and often is. But nothing in science can give you the love, grace, mercy, peace, and joy that come from knowing God. For that . . . you need *faith*.

◆ What are some of your favorite things in the natural world (trees, flowers, rivers, animals)? How do they reflect God's creativity, intentionality, and brilliance?

◆ How has your view of science changed since reading chapter 9 in *The Benefit of Doubt* and completing this lesson? What impact has this had on your faith?

◆ When have you recently noticed something in the natural world—a sunrise, an eclipse, ocean waves, puppies and kittens, thunder and lightning, whatever it was—that declared the glory of God for you in that moment?

◆ What is an area of science that currently intrigues you? (It might be astronomy or physics, biology or medicine, geology or meteorology.) Choose one and then spend some time this week doing some research both online and, if possible, in person by talking to a scientist, doctor, researcher, or other expert. Make note of which of your discoveries within this field point back to God.

NOTES

1. "Scopes Trial," Encyclopedia Britannica, August 29, 2024, https://www.britannica.com/event/Scopes-Trial.

2. "Scopes Trial," History.com, July 10, 2024, https://www.history.com/topics/roaring-twenties/scopes-trial.

3. "Scopes Trial," History.com.

4. Patricia O'Grady, "Thales of Miletus," Internet Encyclopedia of Philosophy, https://iep.utm.edu/thales/.

5. "Ptolemaic System," Encyclopedia Britannica, https://www.britannica.com/science/Ptolemaic-system.

6. "Luminiferous Aether," Wikipedia.com, https://en.wikipedia.org/wiki/Luminiferous_aether.

WHY WOULD GOD LOVE *ME?*

God loves you not because you are worthy but because you are his.

CRAIG GROESCHEL

When you were born, you learned quickly how to adapt to the way your needs got met. Your parents or caregivers made sure you received food, clean diapers, and a warm place to sleep. They also tried to meet your emotional needs for love, comfort, safety, and stability. From the time you were an infant, you began looking for patterns that got you what you needed, whether that was nourishment or to be held and assured of your parents' or caretakers' love.

These assumptions you formed became the basis of how you learned to get your physical and emotional needs met—what psychologists today call "human attachment." The pioneer usually credited with identifying the basic tenets for how you form such relational attachments is John Bowlby, a British psychiatrist and psychoanalyst who specialized in child development. Bowlby's findings were based on observations he made while working in a psychiatric hospital of the various ways that children interacted with their parents.

Bowlby wondered if the factors that shaped a child's personality were not merely biological but also external—a reaction to their home environment, socioeconomic limitations, and parents' relational style.[1] During the 1950s, he narrowed his focus to mother-child separation issues, building on the work of those such as Konrad Lorenz, and eventually concluded that babies not only rely on their mothers for food but also for security. Soon, other researchers began reaching similar conclusions and tested their hypotheses in studies, including some that separated toddlers from mothers in order to observe their reactions.

As more research has been done, the science of human attachment has become respected as an evidence-based area of therapeutic study and treatment. Attachment science provides insight into the default patterns of relating that people form in childhood and continue into adulthood. It helps individuals grow in self-awareness so they can change unhealthy ways of relating and instead establish healthy relationships with loved ones.

Attachment science can also help us understand some of our attitudes and assumptions in our relationship with God. While we have long accepted the way our earthly parents—particularly our fathers—can influence the way we view God as our heavenly Father, we are now realizing that our responses to our parents may impact our relationship with God just as much. So, for instance, if you wonder how God could possibly love you, it may have something to do with how you learned—or *didn't* learn—to form relational attachments.

◆ Do you tend to need close connections and frequent communication with the people you love, or are you more independent and emotionally self-sufficient? How does this tendency manifest in the way you relate to God?

◆ How much do you already know about attachment science? What have you learned about the ways you typically form connections with others?

◆ How often do you wonder about God's love for you? Why do you think it can sometimes be difficult to believe that God can know *everything* about you and still love you?

◆ When you consider how you were loved imperfectly by your earthly parents, how has that influenced the way you experience God's love?

EXPLORING THE TRUTH

Attachment science continues to confirm the truth found in Scripture. When God created the first human, Adam, in his own image, he stated that it was not good for this creation to be alone. Adam needed someone similar to himself with whom to connect. So God created another human in his own image, Eve, to accompany Adam.

As you will recall, God also gave Adam and Eve the gift of free will, which opened the door to their sinful choice to disobey him. Ever since, this tendency toward sin has remained part of the human condition. While sin manifests itself in many ways and results in a variety of consequences, relationships often reveal how our sin can have ripple effects. Simply put, people who have been hurt often hurt others.

The relational and emotional wounds we've experienced contribute to how we view our need for others—and our view of our relationship with God. Depending on how we experienced love growing up, or didn't experience it, we may struggle to believe that we are worth loving. Complicating the problem is that we tend to learn that love is based on the value of who or what is being loved. This kind of conditional love relies on *merit*.

So, for instance, when you were well-behaved and conformed to your parents' ideas of being a good son or daughter, you probably felt loved by them. This reinforced the idea that your *good behavior* led to their love. But if you misbehaved, or didn't excel in academics, or caused your parents problems, you received discipline and didn't feel so loved by them. This, in turn, reinforced the idea that your *bad behavior* led to them not loving you.

Now, hopefully your parents or caregivers were of the kind who made sure you knew you were loved even when you misbehaved. They told you that you were loved simply because you were their kid, and you understood their love for you didn't depend on your performance. But even in this ideal case, your parents still did not love you *perfectly*. They made mistakes and gave you faulty information about love. After all, they were still flawed human beings.

Perhaps you've heard people say, "My parents loved me the best they could." This may indeed be true—but it's still lacking. God's love for you, however, is complete and without lack. It is based on the fact that he loves you simply because you belong to him—you are "his kid." He loves you not because of anything you do, or have done, or because of any ability you possess.

God loves you *perfectly*. He sees you as precious and valuable to him—so valuable, in fact, that he gave up what was most valuable and precious to him. "But God demonstrates his own love for us in this: While we were still sinners, Christ died for us" (Romans 5:8).

> [35] *Who shall separate us from the love of Christ? Shall trouble or hardship or persecution or famine or nakedness or danger or sword? . . .* [37] *No, in all these things we are more than conquerors through him who loved us.* [38] *For I am convinced that neither death nor life, neither angels nor demons, neither the present nor the future, nor any powers,* [39] *neither height nor depth, nor anything else in all creation, will be able to separate us from the love of God that is in Christ Jesus our Lord.*
>
> **ROMANS 8:35, 37–39**

◆ What were some ways you experienced performance-based love growing up? What did you have to do, say, or be in order to feel like you were loved?

◆ Who is someone you love solely for who he or she is and not because of what that person does or gives to you? How does this reflect the way God loves you?

◆ How can false assumptions and inaccurate views of your worth result in doubts about God's love? When have you experienced this recently?

◆ How do you *know* that God loves you? What is your basis for knowing that God's love for you is unconditional?

QUESTIONING THE TRUTH

Another reason why people often doubt that God loves them is because of how sinful they view themselves to be. Their thinking goes something like this: *I have done so many things wrong in my life and am so far gone that God could not possibly love someone like me.* Even at first glance, such a view is clearly false because it put limits on God. Do we really believe that an all-powerful God can't love us or do anything with our lives because of our past mistakes?

When we doubt that God could possibly love us because of our sins, we are either misunderstanding his love or are overlooking its totality. The Bible states that God's love not only gives us value as his beloved children but also covers our sins. And not just some of them—but *all* of them. As Peter wrote, "Love covers a multitude of sins" (1 Peter 4:8 ESV).

If you wonder what this means—how God's love can cover a multitude of your sins—just imagine you are about to pay your monthly bills when you discover you have no money. You panic and call your bank, your landlord, your credit card company, your utility company, and everyone else you owe. But each time the person answers your call, you are told you owe *nothing*—your bills have all been paid. And not just for this month . . . but forever!

You could not possibly hope to pay the debt of your sins. As Paul wrote, "the wages of sin is death" (Romans 6:23), and that is exactly what you have collected. So Jesus paid the debt for you—and for everyone else. His death and resurrection made it possible for the penalty of our sins to be satisfied once and for all. "This is how God showed his love among us: He sent his one and only Son into the world that we might live through him. This is love: not that we loved God, but that he loved us and sent his Son as an atoning sacrifice for our sins" (1 John 4:9–10).

When you put your faith in Jesus' sacrifice, he *atones* for your sins, which means that he *covers* them. You employ the same idea today when you say to a friend, "Let me give you twenty dollars to *cover* the bill." The bill has been covered and paid, and now no one can hold the debt against you. The love of God has removed your sins as far as the east is from the west (see Psalm 103:12). No matter what you've done or left undone, said or you wish you could take back, or whom you've hurt and how you've hurt them, your sins cannot prevent God from loving you.

◆ When have you felt that your struggles with sin have prevented God from loving you? What thoughts and feelings swirled inside you during those times?

◆ What does it mean for God's love to *cover* the multitude of your sins? How does that affect your ability to trust him and walk by faith?

◆ What aspects of your past make it hard for you to believe that God is willing to forgive all your sins? Do you find it easier to believe that God could forgive others but not you? Explain your response.

◆ What would your life look like if you were completely secure in the fullness of God's love? What is standing in the way of you having this kind of confidence in his love?

DIGGING DEEPER INTO DOUBT

Love is not just a characteristic of God. Love is who he is. "God is love. Whoever lives in love lives in God, and God in them" (1 John 4:16). You might think of yourself as a loving person, but as a human being, you will have your non-loving moments. Because, well, you're human.

However, God is not only loving but is also love in its purest form and essence. This means he is *always* loving—there is never a moment when he isn't love. What does God's love look like? As Paul described it, "[God's] love is patient [and] kind. It does not envy, it does not boast, it is not proud. It does not dishonor others, it is not self-seeking, it is not easily angered, it keeps no record of wrongs. [God's] love does not delight in evil but rejoices with the truth. It always protects, always trusts, always hopes, always perseveres" (1 Corinthians 13:4–7).

When you begin to truly experience this type of love that comes from God, you begin to love differently as well. You grow in your ability to love others as God loves you.

So . . . to reinforce the point, God *is* love, and his love for you is unconditional. It is not based on you meeting his standards. While he loves you too much to allow you to remain in your sin, he doesn't require that you "get yourself cleaned up" before he can love you. He loves you when you meet the standard and loves you the same when you don't meet it. You can't earn his love, and you can't sin your way out of it. There is nothing you can do to make him love you more and nothing you can do to make him love you less.

In fact, you can never be more loved than you are right now.

◆ When have you been the most convinced of God's love for you? Why can you be even more confident in his love for you right now?

◆ How have your experiences with the way people have loved you in the past interfered with your experience of the way God loves you today? How would you describe the difference between the way people love and the way God loves?

◆ How has the love of God empowered you to love beyond your human capacity? When have you been able to love others in this way recently?

◆ When you consider Paul's description of love in 1 Corinthians 13:4–7, which qualities stand out to you? Which ones do you want to cultivate more intentionally in your life?

DOUBTFUL AT BEST

Your doubts do not define you—they lead you back to love. When you can move past your doubts and accept God's love for you, it will turn your life from upside down to right side up. You can see examples of this in the lives of the disciples. In some ways, Peter remained the impulsive fisherman he was when Jesus first called to him. Yet through the course of their time together and the way Jesus loved, Peter realized that even when he failed—even when he denied knowing Jesus—the Lord still loved him unconditionally.

Or consider John. Jesus invited John to follow him, but he didn't do so because John was educated, highly motivated, or successful. In fact, Jesus called him and his brother, James, the "sons of thunder" (Mark 3:17), which implies they were a bit rough around the edges. But over the course of John spending time with Jesus, he became known as "the disciple whom Jesus loved" (John 13:23; 19:26; 21:7). John rested his head on Jesus' shoulder during the final meal the disciples ate together before Christ was arrested later that night (see John 13:23).

John went from being a rowdy rabble-rouser to being a man transformed by the love of God. John's past didn't define him, his old reputation didn't define him, and his mistakes didn't define him. Rather, he was defined *as the one Jesus loved*. The same is true of you! No matter what others have said about you, or how your family views you, or how the kids at school made you feel, or what your boss says, none of that defines you. *You are the one Jesus loves.*

Jesus not only loves you but he came to rescue you. He said, "I am the good shepherd; I know my sheep and my sheep know me" (John 10:14). Jesus also said, "If a man owns a hundred sheep, and one of them wanders away, will he not leave the ninety-nine on the hills and go to look for the one that wandered off? And if he finds it, truly I tell you, he is happier about that one sheep than about the ninety-nine that did not wander off" (Matthew 18:12–13). So even if you "wander off," you remain secure in the love of the Good Shepherd. He loves the missing one the same as the ninety-nine in the flock. He misses you and wants you back.

If you have wandered away from him—if your doubts have dragged you away from the flock—know that he misses you and is coming to find you. You are not insignificant to him. You are not too sinful for him to save. *You are the one Jesus loves.*

◆ How has addressing your doubts in this study increased your awareness of God's love? How would you describe your experience now of being loved by God?

◆ What are some of the ways your life has changed since you first started following Jesus? What caused or contributed to these changes?

◆ When you say out loud, "I am the one Jesus loves," what feelings rise up inside you? How are you growing in your awareness of how much Christ loves you?

◆ What is your biggest takeaway from completing this workbook? How has addressing your questions strengthened your faith and enriched your relationship with God?

NOTE
1. "What Is Attachment Theory?" The Attachment Project, https://www.attachmentproject.com/attachment-theory/.

GIVING GOD
THE BENEFIT OF
THE DOUBT

When you give God the benefit of the doubt, you also experience the benefit of doubt.

As you've learned, not only is it completely normal to have doubts, but your doubts can actually lead you into a closer relationship with God. However, for your doubts to strengthen your faith, you have to avoid falling into one of two extremes: (1) denying your faith, or (2) denying your questions. Instead, you need to choose another option.

We see this third option demonstrated in the Old Testament story of Job. After Job lost everything, he began to question God. Yet even in the midst of all his pain, confusion, anger, and sadness, he *gave God the benefit of the doubt*. Distraught from unbearable loss, Job held on to his faith and declared, "Though he slay me, yet will I hope in him" (Job 13:15), and, "I know that my redeemer lives, and that in the end he will stand on the earth" (19:25).

Job had doubts, just as we would have if we went through what he experienced. Yet he didn't allow those doubts to define the way that he viewed God. He continued to trust in the Lord, even though he couldn't understand why he was having to endure everything that he was suffering. Job had already decided what he believed about God and their relationship. And because he had already made that decision, when the hard times came that caused him to doubt, he knew it didn't mean that he had to give up on God.

You can make that same faith-filled decision to give God the benefit of the doubt. The decision won't mean that things will get better right away or that you won't continue to struggle at times. But if you choose to pursue God one day at a time, he will take you to a place of greater trust, stronger faith, and deeper intimacy with him than you've ever had before.

And that's the benefit of doubt.

LEADER'S GUIDE

This workbook is a companion to *The Benefit of Doubt* and is designed for both individuals and groups. If you're participating in a group that has designated you as its leader, thank you for agreeing to serve in this capacity. What you have chosen to do is valuable and will make a great difference in the lives of others.

The Benefit of Doubt is a ten-lesson study built around individual completion of this workbook and small-group interaction. As the group leader, think of yourself as the host of a dinner party. Your job is to take care of your guests by managing all the behind-the-scenes details so that when everyone arrives, they can just enjoy their time together.

As group leader, your role is not to answer all the questions or reteach the content—the book, this workbook, and the Holy Spirit will do most of that work. Your job is to guide the experience and create an environment where people can process, question, and reflect—not necessarily receive more instruction.

Make sure everyone in the group gets a copy of the workbook. This will keep everyone on the same page and help the process run more smoothly. If some group members are unable to purchase the workbook, arrange it so that people can share the resource with other group members. Giving everyone access to all the material will position this study to be as rewarding an experience as possible. Everyone should feel free to write in their workbooks and bring them to group every week.

SETTING UP THE GROUP

As the group leader, you'll want to create an environment that encourages sharing and learning. A church sanctuary or formal classroom may not be as ideal as a living room, because those locations can feel formal and less intimate. No matter what setting you choose, provide enough comfortable seating for everyone, and, if possible, arrange the seats in a circle. This will make group interaction and conversation more efficient and natural.

Also, try to get to the meeting site early so you can greet participants as they arrive. Simple refreshments create a welcoming atmosphere and can be a wonderful addition to a group-study evening. Try to take food and pet allergies into account to make your guests as comfortable as possible. You may also want to consider offering childcare to those with children who want to attend. Managing these details up front will make the rest of your group experience flow smoothly and provide a welcoming space in which to engage the content of *The Benefit of Doubt*.

STARTING YOUR GROUP TIME

Once everyone has arrived, it's time to begin the group. Here are some simple tips to make your group time healthy, enjoyable, and effective.

First, consider beginning the meeting with a short prayer, and remind the group members to put their phones on silent. This is a way to make sure you can all be present with one another and with God. Then, give each person one or two minutes to check in before diving into the material.

In your first session, participants can introduce themselves and share what they hope to experience in this group study. Beginning with your second session, people may need more time to share their insights from their personal studies and to enjoy getting better acquainted.

As you begin going through the material, invite members to share their experiences and discuss their responses with the group. Usually, you won't answer the discussion questions yourself, but you may need to go first a couple of times and set an example, answering briefly and with a reasonable amount of transparency. You may also want to help participants debrief and process what they're learning as they complete each session individually ahead of each group meeting. Debriefing something like this is a bit different from responding to questions about the material because the content comes from their real lives. The basic experiences that you want the group to reflect on are:

- *What was the best part about this week's lesson?*
- *What was the hardest part?*
- *What did I learn about myself?*
- *What did I learn about God?*

LEADING THE DISCUSSION TIME

Encourage all the group members to participate in the discussion, but make sure they know they don't have to do so. As the discussion progresses, you may want to follow up with comments such as, "Tell me more about that," or, "Why did you answer that way?" This will allow the group participants to deepen their reflections and invite meaningful sharing in a nonthreatening way.

While each lesson in this workbook includes multiple sections, you do not have to go through each section and cover every question or exercise. Feel free to go with the dynamic in the group and skip around if needed to cover all the material more naturally. You can pick and choose questions based on either the needs of your group or how the conversation is flowing. Also, don't be afraid of silence. Offering a question and allowing up to thirty seconds of silence is okay. It allows people space to think about how they want to respond and also gives them time to do so.

As group leader, you are the boundary keeper for your group. Do not let anyone (yourself included) dominate the group time. Keep an eye out for group members who might be tempted to "attack" folks they disagree with or try to "fix" those having struggles. These kinds of behaviors can derail a group's momentum, so they need to be steered in a different direction. Model active listening and encourage everyone in your group to do the same. This will make your group time a safe space and create a positive community.

At the end of each group session, encourage the participants to take just a few minutes to review what they've learned and write down one or two key takeaways. This will help them cement the big ideas in their minds as you close the session. Close your time together with prayer as a group.

Remember to have fun. Spending time with others and growing closer to God is a gift to enjoy and embrace. And get ready for God to change your thinking and change your life.

Thank you again for taking the time to lead your group. You are making a difference in the lives of others and having an impact on how they see the benefit of doubt.

ABOUT THE AUTHOR

Craig Groeschel is a *New York Times* bestselling author and the found-
ing and senior pastor of Life.Church, which created the free YouVersion
Bible App and is one of the largest churches in the world. He has written
twenty books and hosts the top-ranking *Craig Groeschel Leadership Podcast.*
As a widely respected leader in the church, Craig speaks frequently at
leadership events and conferences worldwide. Craig and his wife, Amy,
live in Oklahoma. Connect with Craig at www.craiggroeschel.com.

Doubt Isn't a Dead End

Find free, honest, and helpful resources at
finds.life.church

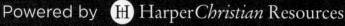